LIVING IN LOVE
CHANGING OUR WORLD

LIVING IN LOVE
CHANGING OUR WORLD

JOIE FROELICH

AgapeDeo Publishing

Copyright 2019 © by Joie Froelich

All rights reserved. Written permission must be secured from the publisher to use or reproduce any part of this book, except for a brief excerpt included by a reviewer as part of a written newspaper, magazine, website, or journal review.

All Scripture verses are taken from the New International Version (NIV) unless otherwise specifically noted. The Holy Bible, New International Version®, NIV® Copyright ©1973, 1978, 1984, 2011 by Biblica, Inc.® Used by permission. All rights reserved worldwide.

Scriptures marked (NKJV). Scripture taken from The New King James Version®. Copyright © 1982 by Thomas Nelson. Used by permission. All rights reserved.

Scripture quotations marked (NLT) are taken from The Holy Bible, New Living Translation, copyright© 1996, 2004, 2007, 2013 by Tyndale House Foundation. Used by permission of Tyndale House Publishers Inc., Carol Stream, Illinois 60188. All rights reserved.

ISBN 978-1-7335843-0-2

Library of Congress Control Number: 2019901961

Published by AgapeDeo Publishing
A Division of Living In Love Ministry
223 Willoughby Way East
Minnetonka, MN 55305

Print books may be available for purchase in bulk quantities for promotional or group use. To request information on discounts and terms, please contact the publisher or visit our website at: www.livinginloveministry.com

Dedication

This book is dedicated to my dear friend, Donna Glenn.
Our loving and gracious Lord changed my life through you.
I am forever grateful.

Table of Contents

CHAPTER ONE 1
THE IMPORTANCE OF LOVE

CHAPTER TWO 17
LOVE THAT CHANGES LIVES

CHAPTER THREE 29
WHAT TRUE LOVE IS

CHAPTER FOUR 51
LOVE WITH DIVINE HELP

CHAPTER FIVE 71
THE ATTITUDES AND ATTRIBUTES OF LIVING IN LOVE

CHAPTER SIX 89
LOVE IN ACTION

CHAPTER SEVEN 115
LOVE: A COMMAND AND A COMMISSION

Acknowledgements 129

Thank You To My Readers 131

CHAPTER ONE

THE IMPORTANCE OF LOVE

THERE IS NOTHING MORE ESSENTIAL TO life than love. It is love that gives purpose and meaning to our lives. Love encourages us, enables us, gives us hope, strengthens us, builds us up, sustains us, heals us, and restores us. Love moves us to acts of great courage and extraordinary sacrifice. Love lifts us up in the face of overwhelming fear and makes it possible to endure otherwise unbearable pain. Love brings us exquisite joy and unsurpassed peace. Love fulfills us and is our true reason for living. We could not survive without love – because love is the very essence of life.

There is rarely a day that goes by we don't hear one of the many and varied stories of love's powerful impact on life. Beautiful and colorful love stories abound. We delight in stories of people falling in love, of deep, lifelong friendships, and of those who overcome tremendous obstacles and enormous odds for love. We feel a mixture of sorrow, pride, and awe when we hear the profoundly moving stories of those who make incomparable sacrifices for love. Such accounts include people who gave up their own life to save the life of a cherished loved one or friend; or as in the many heart-rending stories of 9/11, those who selflessly sacrificed their lives for the lives of people they had never even met.

Unfortunately, as we know only too well, not all the stories we hear are about people who feel the love of someone special in their lives, or perhaps of anyone at all. We have all seen the heartache, despair, and loneliness that affect so many people in our world today. The daily news is full of tragic stories of those who feel unwanted, unloved, and hopeless. Too many people have taken their own lives or have taken the lives of others. In virtually every one of these circumstances, the root cause of these painful tragedies stems from love, or more specifically, the loss or lack thereof. When love is absent in someone's life, it can have devastating, if not deadly, consequences.

Few stories convey with more startling clarity just how critical love's impact on life is than the early 1990s news reports that revealed a heartbreaking look at why infants and children were dying in Romanian orphanages. Journalists found that the children in these orphanages were fed and clothed, but spent their young lives in cold, stark cribs without receiving any form of affection, tenderness, or nurturing. No one held them close or cuddled them. There were no hugs, no tender kisses on their small soft cheeks, and no gentle hand to wipe away their tears. There was no loving human touch at all. As a result, these helpless children became lethargic, unresponsive, and their tiny bodies systematically shut down until they died. This senseless loss of life is known as nonorganic Failure to Thrive syndrome, or simply stated, the lack of human love and affection. While this story brought to light the harsh realities of this syndrome, it is not exclusive to these orphanages in Romania. It occurs right here where we live, taking the lives of children, as well as adults, who have no love in their lives. In varying circumstances, for various reasons, there are people who quite literally are dying for love, or more specifically, the lack of it, every day.

THE IMPORTANCE OF LOVE

We cannot live without love because it is a fundamental need within every human heart to both love and be loved. It is this inherent need within us that makes love so essential to life. It is, very simply, the way every one of us is created.

CREATED TO LOVE

In Genesis, the first book in the Bible, it states, "God created man in his own image, in the image of God he created him; male and female he created them" (Genesis 1:27). What is this image of God in which we have all been made? The apostle John's answer is unequivocal: "God is love" (1 John 4:16). Humankind, then, was created in the likeness of God – who *is* love. We are created out of love, by the Creator who is love, to be creatures of love. We are, therefore, created with the inherent need and desire both to love and be loved. By God's own design we are meant to live in loving relationship with Him and with one another.

PERFECT LOVE FOR IMPERFECT PEOPLE

Adam and Eve, the first man and woman God created, walked in perfect love with their Creator. Their love was pure, boundless, and full of joy. It knew only goodness, kindness, patience, faithfulness, honesty, and caring. It was flawless. Even so, cunning and full of evil deceit, Satan successfully tempted Adam and Eve into sin. As a result, the perfect love they had known was lost, and their sin led to the sinful, fallen nature of all humankind. No one since Adam and Eve's fall has been born without a sinful nature. Consequently, instead of an infinite life of perfect love, humankind was now condemned to live in a broken world filled with sin, suffering, and sorrow until ultimately succumbing to death, eternal separation from God, and eternity in hell.

Humankind's fall, however, did not in any way change the nature of God. God is and always will be love. He will always love us, even while in His perfection He hates our sin. It grieved our Creator's heart that we should be separated from Him. As a Father who loves His children, God wants to share His love with us for all eternity. Nevertheless, because He is holy, and we are sinful, God cannot bring us to be with Him unless we can be made pure again, unless we are redeemed. Knowing that as sinful human beings, we can never restore ourselves to holiness, God, in His infinite love, sent His own Son to save us. The apostle John tells us, "This is how God showed his love among us: He sent his one and only Son into the world that we might live through him. This is love: not that we loved God, but that he loved us and sent his Son as an atoning sacrifice for our sins" (1 John 4:9-10).

THE ULTIMATE GIFT OF LOVE

Jesus, the Son of God, who had never sinned, came to earth as a Man and took upon Himself the sins of the world. He endured the punishment that should have belonged to all of us and sacrificed Himself in our place. He suffered brutal torture and died a horrible death nailed to a cross before being raised from the dead and returning to heaven in glory. Because one man's sin brought sin and death to all humankind, God, in His great love and mercy sent one Man, His own Son, to take away the sins of the world so that we might be restored to perfect love with Him once again. The apostle Paul states, "Yes, Adam's one sin brings condemnation for everyone, but Christ's one act of righteousness brings a right relationship with God and new life for everyone. Because one person disobeyed God, many became sinners. But because one other person obeyed God, many will be made righteous" (Romans 5:18-19 NLT).

The God who *is* love made His only begotten Son our substitutionary sacrifice not because we earned it or deserved it, but solely because of His unwavering, unalterable love for us. Our loving, gracious, and merciful heavenly Father provided an escape from certain death and eternal damnation for every person who accepts His Son, Jesus Christ, as their Savior. "The wages of sin is death," attests the apostle Paul, "but the gift of God is eternal life in Christ Jesus our Lord" (Romans 6:23 NKJV). There has never been, nor will there ever be, a greater gift of love!

We receive this priceless gift simply because God loves us. There is nothing we can do to earn it or deserve it; therefore, it is truly a gift of grace. As the apostle Paul explains, "God is so rich in mercy, and he loved us so much, that even though we were dead because of our sins, he gave us life when he raised Christ from the dead. (It is only by God's grace that you have been saved!) For he raised us from the dead along with Christ and seated us with him in the heavenly realms because we are united with Christ Jesus. So God can point to us in all future ages as examples of the incredible wealth of his grace and kindness toward us, as shown in all he has done for us who are united with Christ Jesus. God saved you by his grace when you believed. And you can't take credit for this; it is a gift from God. Salvation is not a reward for the good things we have done, so none of us can boast about it" (Ephesians 2:4-9 NLT).

THE PLAN FOR ETERNAL LOVE

It has always been God's plan that we be His sons and daughters and know the unparalleled love that comes from being members of His family. It gives Him great pleasure to shower us with love, kindness, wisdom, and understanding. His heart's desire is for us to be richly blessed through His Son's sacrifice. "Even before he made the world," writes the apostle Paul, "God loved us and chose us in Christ to be holy and without fault in his eyes. God decided in advance to adopt us into his own family by bringing us to himself through Jesus Christ. This is what he wanted to do, and it gave him great pleasure. So we praise God for the glorious grace he has poured out on us who belong to his dear Son. He is so rich in kindness and grace that he purchased our freedom with the blood of his Son and forgave our sins. He has showered his kindness on us, along with all wisdom and understanding" (Ephesians 1:4-8 NLT).

Without question, the greatest demonstration of God's immutable nature and the depth of His unfailing love for us is found in the sacrifice of His only begotten Son, Jesus Christ. In what is one of the most well-known verses in all of Scripture, Jesus conveys the incomparable depth of His Father's unconditional love for us when He declares, "God so loved the world that he gave his one and only Son, that whoever believes in him shall not perish but have eternal life" (John 3:16).

Jesus was and is the infinite fullness of God's love. His sacrifice brings us together with Him into the unfailing grace of God's perfect love. When we accept Jesus as our Savior, we are bound together with Him in an eternal love relationship with God. As such, we are also bound to live by the commandments of love He gives to us. It is through these commandments, and through God's Word and Jesus' example, that we learn how to live in true love and genuine joy. Our Lord and Savior's greatest desire for us is that we know the joy of remaining in God's love forever. "As the Father has loved me, so have I loved you," Jesus tells us. "Now remain in my love. If you keep my commands, you will remain in my love, just as I have kept my Father's commands and remain in his love. I have told you this so that my joy may be in you and that your joy may be complete" (John 15:9-11).

TO LOVE IS THE GREATEST COMMANDMENT

So, what are the commands we need to obey to remain in God's love and to know the joy that Jesus knew? Jesus Himself gives us the answer as He responds to a question in an interview with the Sadducees and Pharisees, the men of His time who were considered experts in the laws of Scripture.

"'Of all the commandments, which is the most important?' [asked one of the teachers of the law.]

"The most important one," answered Jesus, "is this: ... 'Love the Lord your God with all your heart and with all your soul and with all your mind and with all your strength.' The second is this: 'Love your neighbor as yourself.' There is no commandment greater than these" (Mark 12:28-31).

Jesus further defines the importance of these two great commandments when He states, "All the Law and the Prophets hang on these two commandments" (Matthew 22:40). All the Law (every command given in Scripture) and the words of the prophets, Jesus said, are fulfilled if we keep these two commandments to love. In addition to the Ten Commandments most of us are familiar with, there are over 600 commands recorded in the Bible. Yet, Jesus tells us that we are obeying them all when we obey these two commandments to love. In an unmistakable way, Jesus is telling us that there is nothing more important in life than living in love.

LOVE FOR GOD

In the first and greatest commandment, Jesus instructs, "Love the Lord your God with all your heart and with all your soul and with all your mind and with all your strength" (Mark 12:30). Our Lord and Savior is asking us to love God with our entire being: our whole heart – that is, above all else, deeply, passionately, and completely; with our entire mind – seeking to know Him to the fullest extent possible and growing in knowledge, wisdom, and understanding of His Word; with all our soul – faithfully committed to Him, and seeking His presence continually and prayerfully; and with the totality of our strength – making Him our first priority every day, and being thoroughly committed to Him in every way. God wants to be our first and greatest love.

If you have ever been "head-over-heels" in love, you know it is all-consuming, deeply personal, and intensely passionate. The one we love fills our heart night and day. They are always on our mind, and we can't seem to know enough about them or spend enough time in their presence. We willingly do everything possible to show them how much we love and care for them. This is precisely how our heavenly Father wants us to love Him!

OBEDIENCE IS AN ACT OF LOVE

Our Lord also wants us to understand that our obedience to the two greatest commandments is, in and of itself, an act of love for Him. Jesus tells us, "If you love me, obey my commandments ... Those who accept my commandments and obey them are the ones who love me" (John 14:15, 21 NLT). John, Jesus' beloved disciple, affirms, "Everyone who believes that Jesus is the Christ has become a child of God. And everyone who loves the Father loves his children, too. We know we love God's children if we love God and obey his commandments" (1 John 5:1-2 NLT).

LOVE FOR OUR NEIGHBORS

For each one of us who have genuinely come to know God and the depth of His love for us, it is impossible for us not to love Him. Likewise, having a personal relationship with our Lord and Savior, Jesus Christ, would not be possible without first understanding the depth of His love for us when He laid down His life to save us and loving Him in return. Loving Jesus in return means sharing His love with others – all those He defines as our neighbors. The apostle John states simply and eloquently: "We love because He first loved us" (1 John 4:19).

John further explains the unique relationship between God's love for us and our love for others in one of his most beautiful, compelling, and timeless letters. "Dear friends," writes the apostle, "let us continue to love one another, for love comes from God. Anyone who loves is a child of God and knows God. But anyone who does not love does not know God, for God is love. God showed how much he loved us by sending his one and only Son into the world so that we might have eternal life through him. This is real love—not that we loved God, but that he loved us and sent his Son as a sacrifice to take away our sins. Dear friends, since God loved us that much, we surely ought to love each other" (1 John 4:7-11 NLT).

The apostle Paul, in one of his letters to the church in Rome, explains the meaning and importance of obeying the second greatest commandment this way: "Let no debt remain outstanding, except the continuing debt to love one another, for whoever loves others has fulfilled the law. The commandments, 'You shall not commit adultery,' 'You shall not murder,' 'You shall not steal,' 'You shall not covet,' and whatever other commandments there may be, are summed up in this one command: 'Love your neighbor as yourself.' Love does no harm to its neighbor. Therefore love is the fulfillment of the law" (Romans 13:8-10).

ENEMIES ARE NEIGHBORS TOO

When most of us think of loving our neighbors, we often have in mind the people we know and care about – our friends, family members, fellow believers, co-workers, and perhaps even a few acquaintances. However, our Lord has a far broader range of people in mind when He issues the commandment to love our neighbors as ourselves. When asked by one of the legal experts who He considers to be a neighbor, Jesus responds with the following illustration:

"A Jewish man was traveling from Jerusalem down to Jericho, and he was attacked by bandits. They stripped him of his clothes, beat him up, and left him half dead beside the road. By chance a priest came along. But when he saw the man lying there, he crossed to the other side of the road and passed him by. A Temple assistant walked over and looked at him lying there, but he also passed by on the other side.

"Then a despised Samaritan [Jews and Samaritans were hated enemies] came along, and when he saw the man, he felt compassion for him. Going over to him, the Samaritan soothed his wounds with olive oil and wine and bandaged them. Then he put the man on his own donkey and took him to an inn, where he took care of him. The next day he handed the innkeeper two silver coins, telling him, 'Take care of this man. If his bill runs higher than this, I'll pay you the next time I'm here.'

"'Now which of these three would you say was a neighbor to the man who was attacked by bandits?' Jesus asked.

"The man replied, 'The one who showed him mercy.'

"Then Jesus said, 'Yes, now go and do the same'" (Luke 10:30-37 NLT, emphasis mine).

Our neighbors, in the eyes of our Lord and Savior, include anyone and everyone who comes across our path. It makes no difference whether we know them or like them, whether they are kind and caring or cruel and hurtful. It doesn't matter whether they are fellow believers or unbelievers. And, as reflected in the above story of the good Samaritan, our neighbors also include our enemies.

Our Lord Jesus leaves no room for doubt when He states definitively, "To you who are listening I say: Love your enemies, do good to those who hate you, bless those who curse you, pray for those who mistreat you ... If you love those who love you, what credit is that to you? Even sinners love those who love them. And if you do good to those who are good to you, what credit is that to you? Even sinners do that. And if you lend to those from whom you expect repayment, what credit is that to you? Even sinners lend to sinners, expecting to be repaid in full. But love your enemies, do good to them, and lend to them without expecting to get anything back. Then your reward will be great, and you will be children of the Most High, because he is kind to the ungrateful and wicked. Be merciful, just as your Father is merciful" (Luke 6:27-28, 32-36).

Our Lord's directive to love, do good, bless, pray for, and be merciful to those who have hurt us is often extremely difficult, if not impossible, for us to do in our own strength – especially when we, or those we love or care for, have been grossly mistreated or grievously harmed by someone. In such exceptionally challenging and often painful circumstances, we can draw strength from the apostle Paul's powerful reminder: "God demonstrates his own love for us in this: *While we were still sinners, Christ died for us*" (Romans 5:8, emphasis mine).

We are all enemies of God through sin. "*All* have sinned and fall short of the glory of God," declares the apostle Paul (Romans 3:23 NKJV, emphasis mine). The *all* Paul is referring to includes each one of us. As Paul once reminded Titus, his young associate pastor, "At one time we too were foolish, disobedient, deceived and enslaved by all kinds of passions and pleasures. We lived in malice and envy, being hated and hating one another. But when the kindness and love of God our Savior appeared, he saved us, not because of righteous things we had done, but because of his mercy" (Titus 3:3-5). Since our merciful heavenly Father loved us enough to send His Son to die for us while we were still His enemies, how can we stand before Him, thanking Him and telling Him we love Him for what He has done for us, and then refuse to show the same love to our enemies?

Jesus' command to love our neighbors, including our enemies, does not require us to personally like or become friends with every person we meet; nor should we ever accept or condone inappropriate or sinful behavior. However, our Lord does require that we *love the sinner* even while we *hate the sin*. When we find this to be particularly challenging to do, it is helpful to remember that often our most impactful and effective witness for our Lord and Savior occurs as we demonstrate His love toward those who appear to be the least deserving of it. In fact, it may be that sharing our Lord's love with such a person may one day be the very thing the Holy Spirit uses to change their life or open the door for an unbeliever to accept Jesus Christ as their Lord and Savior.

LOVE FOR OURSELVES

Although we seldom focus on the second half of the second greatest commandment, "love your neighbor as yourself," the words *as yourself* are vitally important if we are to obey our Lord's command completely. Having a healthy, God-centered love for ourselves as His divine creation and redeemed children, the brothers and sisters of Christ Jesus and co-heirs with Him in the kingdom of heaven, is an imperative prerequisite to loving our neighbors.

Most of us see ourselves through either the eyes of others or our own self-perception rather than through the eyes of our Creator. That often makes loving ourselves very difficult. We may have had a parent, sibling, or another person who put us down and said or did things to us that diminished or damaged how we perceive our value or self-worth. Or perhaps we see our flaws and failures, humanness, and imperfections as definitive of who we are as individuals. God, however, wants us to see that our true identity ultimately lies in Him. He knows that only when we look at ourselves through His eyes, as His precious creation and beloved children, will we have the right kind of love *for* our self, (as opposed to the love *of* ourselves, which is pride).

Our Creator wants us to see that we are His perfect, one-of-a-kind, living works of art. King David recorded in a song of praise to God: "You [God] created my inmost being; you knit me together in my mother's womb. I praise you because I am fearfully and wonderfully made; your works are wonderful, I know that full well" (Psalm 139:13-14, emphasis mine).

Each one of us is uniquely and perfectly designed by our loving heavenly Father to fulfill His divine purpose. The apostle Paul reminds us, "We are God's masterpiece. He has created us anew in Christ Jesus, so we can do the good things he planned for us long ago" (Ephesians 2:10 NLT).

Not only are we wonderfully designed and masterfully created by the hand of almighty God, but we are also created in His image. Among all of God's vast creation, we alone are created in His image. We, separate from all God's other creatures on earth, have the unique ability to communicate with the Creator of the heavens and earth. We, exclusively, have the capacity to give and receive love. And, as the followers of Christ, we, apart from all others, have the extraordinary distinction of being called God's children. The apostle Paul points out: "The Spirit himself testifies with our spirit that we are God's children. Now if we are children, then we are heirs – heirs of God and co-heirs with Christ" (Romans 8:16-17).

"See what great love the Father has lavished on us, that we should be called children of God! And that is what we are!" exclaims the apostle John (1 John 3:1). When we can see ourselves in this context, as deeply loved, cherished, and valuable children of God, the brothers and sisters of Jesus Christ, it should lead us to have a healthy, God-centered love for ourselves. It should also lead us to genuinely love others because they, too, are of such infinite worth and value to our Creator that He sent His only Son to die for them.

INSEPARABLE LOVE

When we come to understand that we are all connected through God's love, that we were all created to live together in His love, we can see that the commandments to love God, our neighbor, and ourselves are inseparable. Loving God means loving all God's people, including ourselves. In our lives on earth, it is through sharing God's love that His love is made complete. The apostle John explains, "Dear friends, since God so loved us, we also ought to love one another. No one has ever seen God; but if we love one another, God lives in us and his love is made complete in us" (1 John 4:11-12).

NOTHING IS MORE IMPORTANT THAN LOVE

There will never be anything more important in life than love. Nowhere is that made clearer in Scripture than in the following words of the apostle Paul: "If I speak in the tongues of men or of angels, but do not have love, I am only a resounding gong or a clanging cymbal. If I have the gift of prophecy and can fathom all mysteries and all knowledge, and if I have a faith that can move mountains, but do not have love, I am nothing. If I give all I possess to the poor and give over my body to hardship that I may boast, but do not have love, I gain nothing" (1 Corinthians 13:1-3).

These words convey the importance of love more vividly than anything I have ever heard. What an extraordinary phenomenon it would be to speak every one of the more than 7,000 languages on earth, in addition to the language of angels. Yet, Paul tells us that even if we could accomplish such an astonishing feat, without love, we would be doing nothing more than making irritating noises, like incessantly reverberating gongs or clashing cymbals.

It would be nothing short of miraculous to foretell the future (prophesy) with perfect accuracy, understand all the mysteries of life, have knowledge of all things, and a faith that is so strong we could literally move mountains from one continent to another. Nevertheless, Paul tells us that even if we were capable of such extraordinary and supernatural wonders, we would still be "nothing" if we didn't have love.

What if we donated everything we own: home, car, clothes, food, and financial assets right down to our last penny, and then, making the ultimate sacrifice laid down our lives to save others from the flames of a burning building? Well, Paul tells us that in God's eyes we would gain nothing from these actions unless there was genuine love in our heart.

The apostle Paul's words make it unmistakably clear that living in love is more important than anything else we will ever do, have, or become. No matter how great our intellect, abilities, sacrifices, successes, wisdom, knowledge, or faith they are ultimately meaningless if they are not grounded in sincere and genuine love, the unselfish, nurturing, and protective love that cannot be achieved apart from God through faith in Christ Jesus. "If anyone acknowledges that Jesus is the Son of God," declares the apostle John, "God lives in them and they in God. And so we know and rely on the love God has for us. God is love. Whoever lives in love lives in God, and God in them" (1 John 4:15-16).

A Word

"Let love and faithfulness never leave you; bind them around your neck, write them on the tablet of your heart. Then you will win favor and a good name in the sight of God and man" (Proverbs 3:3-4).

And A Prayer

"I pray that you, being rooted and established in love, may have power, together with all the Lord's holy people, to grasp how wide and long and high and deep is the love of Christ, and to know this love that surpasses knowledge – that you may be filled to the measure of all the fullness of God" (Ephesians 3:17-19)

LIVING IN LOVE: CHANGING OUR WORLD

CHAPTER TWO

LOVE THAT CHANGES LIVES

WHEN WE LIVE IN OBEDIENCE to our Lord's commands, the difference we can make in the lives of others by reaching out to them with God's love can be life-changing. We can help those in need; encourage those who are struggling, alone, and afraid; bring comfort and compassion to those who are hurting; offer hope to those who feel hopeless; and most importantly, lead the lost toward Jesus and restore those who have fallen away from Him. All of us, living in God's love together, can help change the face of our world – a world that is without question in grave trouble.

None of us, Christian or not, are exempt from the pain, suffering, trials, and tribulations that come with living in this sinful and fallen world. Men, women, and children from every walk of life, every culture, and every nation on earth are struggling to cope with the difficult and challenging problems of living in these increasingly complex and turbulent times.

Broken hearts and shattered dreams; social, financial, and economic problems; sickness and disease; catastrophic natural disasters; violence, terrorism, and wars impact all of us. And sadly, amid all these trials and tragedies people seem to have become less loving, less kind, less forgiving, and more selfish, self-centered, hard-hearted, and hateful. Far too many people in this fast-paced, me-first, twenty-first-century world seem to have little to no regard for one another and even less regard for God.

In a letter to his young protégé, Timothy, the apostle Paul writes, "There will be terrible times in the last days. People will be lovers of themselves, lovers of money, boastful, proud, abusive, disobedient to their parents, ungrateful, unholy, without love, unforgiving, slanderous, without self-control, brutal, not lovers of the good, treacherous, rash, conceited, lovers of pleasure rather than lovers of God" (2 Timothy 3:1-4). Paul paints a frighteningly accurate picture of our world today!

Each of us is seeing and experiencing the truth of the apostle's words in strikingly personal ways: in our own homes, in our schools, in our workplaces, and even in our places of worship. In the world at large, we see it expressed in unprecedented greed and corruption; in heinous acts of violence, terror, and mass murder; and the unfortunate way much of the world turns a blind eye to the suffering and death of millions of people from poverty, sickness, and starvation. Regrettably, these are only a few examples.

Such callousness, loss of values, self-centeredness, and hatred reflect how insidiously and successfully Satan is gaining ground. His evil, sinful ways have taken root in the hearts of individuals, spread to families, infected societies, infiltrated nations, and now threaten to destroy the world as we know it. Many people today are living in fear of what the future holds, not only for themselves and their families but the world. These can be frightening and uncertain times for people everywhere.

Fortunately, as Christians, we know that we have almighty God on our side; and through His unfailing, unstoppable, all-powerful love He has equipped us to win every battle we face whether it is a personal struggle or a world war.

The unfailing love of God is far greater and far stronger than any trouble or hardship this world can bring our way. He is all-knowing (omniscient), all-powerful (omnipotent), and ever-present (omnipresent). He remains faithful in all His promises to us, and we can count on Him to be with us and to help us through every situation and circumstance of life. The author of Hebrews reminds us, "[God] Himself has said, 'I will never leave you nor forsake you'" (Hebrews 13:5 NKJV, emphasis mine).

"Can anything ever separate us from Christ's love?" asks the apostle Paul. "Does it mean he no longer loves us if we have trouble or calamity, or are persecuted, or hungry, or destitute, or in danger, or threatened with death?" Paul's reassuring answer: "No, despite all these things, overwhelming victory is ours through Christ, who loved us. And I am convinced that nothing can ever separate us from God's love. Neither death nor life, neither angels nor demons, neither our fears for today nor our worries about tomorrow—not even the powers of hell can separate us from God's love. No power in the sky above or in the earth below—indeed, nothing in all creation will ever be able to separate us from the love of God that is revealed in Christ Jesus our Lord" (Romans 8:35, 37-39 NLT).

AMBASSADORS FOR CHRIST

Only God has the power to ultimately change our world: to shape lives, change lives, and save lives. However, He calls upon each one of us, as the faithful followers of Christ Jesus, to be His messengers and the instruments of His love here on earth. You and I are to be His change-agents, His witnesses, and His representatives. We are to demonstrate His loving-kindness and share the message of His saving love with a lost and hurting world. The apostle Paul tells us, "We are therefore Christ's ambassadors, as though God were making his appeal through us" (2 Corinthians 5:20).

To be ambassadors for Christ, to appeal to the world on God's behalf, is the most critical calling any of us will ever receive. We are representatives of the Savior of the world and delegates of almighty God. Through us, others can come to know and experience our Lord's extraordinary goodness, grace, mercy, and love.

Understanding the powerful impact and the enormous responsibility of our role as Christ Jesus' ambassadors, we must bear in mind that *everything* an ambassador says and does is representative of the person or party that delegates him or her to represent them. As ambassadors for Christ Jesus, we represent Him in everything we do and say, regardless of where we are, what we are doing, or who happens to see us. Therefore, it is imperative that our conduct is, at all times, and in all circumstances, appropriate to the high calling we have received. We must strive to be a positive reflection of the One who called us, because how well we represent Him has eternal consequences for us, and for every person whose life is touched by ours.

Recognizing the profound significance and exceptional importance of our role as ambassadors for Christ and emissaries of almighty God, the apostle Paul states, "I urge you to live a life worthy of the calling you have received" (Ephesians 4:1). Each of us must ask ourselves if we are living a life worthy of our calling. Do our lives bring honor and glory to God? Are we representing our Lord and Savior in a manner that reflects who He is, rather than how worldly we are? Do people who are suffering and alone see His loving-kindness, caring concern, and compassion reaching out to them through us? Is Jesus' love shining so brightly through us that others long to feel His embrace in their own lives? Does His joy emanate so radiantly from us that people can't wait to find out how we can be so joyful when life can be so hard? Do the hopeless see the hope we have in Him? Do His kindness, patience, and gentleness reach out through us to calm the troubled and soothe their fears? Are we demonstrating His forgiveness and showing others the path to His peace? Are we leading the lost toward eternal life by living constantly and consistently in God's love?

IMITATORS OF GOD AND FOLLOWERS OF CHRIST JESUS

The apostle John tells us, "No one has ever seen God. But if we love each other, God lives in us, and his love is brought to full expression in us" (1 John 4:12 NLT). All true believers, including you and I, are to be the body of God's love here on earth. We are to be His heart – filled with compassion and loving-kindness; His mind – full of wisdom and discernment; His voice – speaking the Truth in love; His hands – reaching out to those in need; His arms – embracing the weak and lifting them up, and; His feet – walking in love and spreading the gospel message.

We are God's representatives to the world and one another. Through us, others can come to know the extraordinary love of God, His goodness, grace, and mercy. As children of God and ambassadors for Christ, we must say and do everything in a spirit of love, with a truly loving heart. Every time we talk to someone we are speaking to them as extensions of God; and our actions, whether witnessed by a casual observer or seen on a public stage, are a direct reflection of His love through us. As such, it is imperative that our conversations and conduct always convey our Lord's love to everyone who sees us. "Imitate God, therefore, in everything you do, because you are his dear children," implores the apostle Paul. "Live a life filled with love, following the example of Christ" (Ephesians 5:1-2 NLT).

To be an imitator of God is to be a follower of Christ Jesus. And to be a follower of Jesus is to live a life of love: obeying the commandments both to love God and love others. There is, in fact, nothing more significant in identifying us as Jesus' true followers than living in His love and obeying His commands. The apostle John explains, "We can be sure that we know [Jesus] if we obey his commandments. If someone claims, 'I know God,' but doesn't obey God's commandments, that person is a liar and is not living in the truth. But those who obey God's word truly show how completely they love him. That is how we know we are living in him. Those who say they live in God should live their lives as Jesus did" (1 John 2:3-6 NLT, emphasis mine).

WALKING AS JESUS WALKED

As Jesus' true followers, we must obey His commands, follow His example, emulate Him in our lives, walk as He walked, and love as He loved. Ralph Venning, the seventeenth-century writer and pastor, wisely said: "Never call yourself 'Christians' and pretend to walk as if you have Christ for an example, unless men may read that in you which was in Christ: *love*" (emphasis mine). [1]

Unfortunately, as we all know only too well, many people claim to be Christians while their conduct and character are anything but loving or Christlike. The apostle Paul, experiencing a similar problem in his day, did not mince words when he remarked in a letter to his dear friend, Titus: "There are many rebellious people who engage in useless talk and deceive others … Such people claim they know God, but they deny him by the way they live. They are detestable and disobedient, worthless for doing anything good" (Titus 1:10, 16 NLT).

Our actions always give us away. People can easily see whether we practice what we preach, or to borrow a more modern phrase, walk our talk. Just as we form impressions and draw conclusions about people's real character by observing their words relative to their actions, they do the same with us. There is, however, a critical difference for us as Christians because what people see in us is an immediate reflection of Christ Jesus. Consequently, what you and I do or say could mean the difference between someone being drawn closer to their Lord and Savior or driven further away from Him.

---

[1] The Puritans on Loving One Another, The New Commandment Renewed, Ralph Venning (1621-1674), Soli Deo Gloria and Don Kistler, Copyright 1997, pp. 42

We are always, in every situation and circumstance, representatives of Christ Jesus – even when we may think no one is watching us or observing our behavior. Many years ago, a friend emailed me a copy of the following story. It is, regrettably, an all too accurate and realistic portrayal of what can and does happen when we forget our lives are to reflect the love of our Lord and Savior. The story goes like this:

An honest man was being tailgated by a stressed-out woman on a busy boulevard. Suddenly, the light turned yellow just in front of him. He did the right thing, stopping at the crosswalk, even though he could have beaten the red light by accelerating through the intersection.

The tailgating woman hit the roof – and the horn – screaming in frustration as she missed her chance to get through the intersection. As she was still in mid-rant, she heard a tap on her window and looked up into the face of a very serious police officer. The officer ordered her to exit her car with her hands up. He took her to the police station where she was searched, fingerprinted, photographed and placed in a holding cell.

After a couple of hours, a policeman approached the cell and opened the door. She was escorted back to the booking desk where the arresting officer was waiting with her personal effects. He said, "I'm very sorry for this mistake. You see, I pulled up behind your car while you were blowing your horn, flipping off the guy in front of you, cursing a blue streak at him. I noticed the 'Choose Life' license plate holder, the 'What Would Jesus Do' bumper sticker, the 'Follow Me to Sunday School' bumper sticker, and the chrome-plated Christian fish emblem on the trunk. Naturally, I assumed you had stolen the car."[2]

Unfortunately, there are times when the frustrations and stresses of daily life get the best of all of us and our conduct is anything but a reflection of our Lord Jesus and His loving character. Nevertheless, when we act the way the rest of the world acts, *or worse*, our behavior ultimately calls into question whether we are, in fact, faithful followers of Jesus. Considering this, the apostle Paul admonishes, "Examine yourselves to

---

[2] Author unknown

see whether you are in the faith; test yourselves. Do you not realize that Christ Jesus is in you – unless, of course, you fail the test?" (2 Corinthians 13:5).

THE EVIDENCE OF OUR FAITH

The way we live and act, our faith in action, is what ultimately conveys to others our relationship with the Lord. It isn't the title we attach to ourselves or the words we use to describe ourselves that ultimately define us. Instead, we are defined by who we demonstrate ourselves to be through our conduct and character. Jesus uses the following metaphor to explain this, stating, "A good tree can't produce bad fruit, and a bad tree can't produce good fruit. A tree is identified by its fruit. Figs are never gathered from thornbushes, and grapes are not picked from bramble bushes. A good person produces good things from the treasury of a good heart, and an evil person produces evil things from the treasury of an evil heart. What you say flows from what is in your heart" (Luke 6:43-45 NLT).

King Solomon put it this way: "As a face is reflected in water, so the heart reflects the real person" (Proverbs 27:19 NLT). In other words, the proof of our Christian faith and character is not found in what we profess to be, but in how we live what we profess to believe. Our actions will always speak louder than our words. If we claim to be Christians, the sincere, committed, and faithful followers of Jesus Christ, then the way we live our lives must prove it to be true. If not, we will be nothing more than hypocrites and our witness, (and the witness of other Christians), for Christ Jesus will be severely damaged, if not destroyed altogether.

Having said this, we cannot be perfect, and God does not expect us to be; but we do need to try hard to walk as Jesus walked and love as He loved: with kindness, gentleness, patience, forgiveness, faithfulness, wisdom, and integrity. We must continually strive to be humble and honorable; and we absolutely must let go of any of the "holier than thou" hypocritical attitudes that drive people away from us, and by association, away from our Lord and Savior.

The apostle Paul warns: "Be very careful, then, how you live – not as unwise but as wise, making the most of every opportunity, because the days are evil. Therefore do not be foolish, but understand what the Lord's will is" (Ephesians 5:15-17). Our Lord's will is that we love Him with our whole being and that we reflect the light of His love so brightly and present His gospel message with such gracious appeal that those who see and hear us will be irresistibly drawn to Him.

SALT AND LIGHT IN A BROKEN WORLD

Jesus uses the analogy of salt and light to express how He views us as His faithful followers and how He wants the world to see us. "You are the salt of the earth" … "You are the light of the world," declares our Savior. "Let your light so shine before men, that they may see your good works and glorify your Father in heaven" (Matthew 5:13-14, 16 NKJV).

As "the salt of the earth" our words and actions must continually accentuate the appealing flavor of God's loving-kindness, preserve and sustain the truth of His Word, and promote a thirst within others to know the perfect love of their Savior.

As "the light of the world" we must project the illuminating light of Jesus' love into a world darkened by evil so that those still lost in sin may find their way into our Lord's glorious and redeeming presence. The young prophet, Daniel, notes, "Those who are wise will shine like the brightness of the heavens, and those who lead many to righteousness, like the stars forever and ever" (Daniel 12:3).

If we want to lead people to righteousness, we must continually convey Christlike character and demonstrate our Lord's love every day, in every way possible, regardless of what may be going on in the world around us. "Whatever happens," counsels the apostle Paul, "conduct yourselves in a manner worthy of the gospel of Christ" (Philippians 1:27).

OUR TRUE IDENTITY

Loving others – believers and unbelievers, friends as well as enemies – the way Jesus loves us is what ultimately identifies us to the rest of the world as Jesus' faithful followers. "Your love for one another," our Lord points out, "will prove to the world that you are my disciples" (John 13:35 NLT).

As Jesus' devoted followers you and I are to love others, including our enemies, not because of who they are or what they may or may not have done, but because of who we are through the relationship we have with our Lord and Savior.

A NEW COMMAND

Because of our unique relationship with Christ Jesus, and because of our roles as His ambassadors and emissaries of almighty God, we are required not only to love others in the way human beings typically love each other but in a way that far exceeds it. Jesus tells us, "A new command I give you: Love one another. *As I have loved you*, so you must love one another" (John 13:34, emphasis mine).

Our Lord Jesus' "new command" does not supersede or replace the original commandment to love our neighbors; rather, it defines *how* we are to love them: sacrificially, the same way He loved us.

A Word

"To those who have been called, who are loved by God the Father and kept by Jesus Christ: mercy, peace and love be yours in abundance" (Jude 1:1-2).

And A Prayer

"We constantly pray for you, that our God may make you worthy of his calling, and that by his power he may bring to fruition your every desire for goodness and your every deed prompted by faith. We pray this so that the name of our Lord Jesus may be glorified in you, and you in him, according to the grace of our God and the Lord Jesus Christ" (2 Thessalonians 1:11-12).

LIVING IN LOVE: CHANGING OUR WORLD

CHAPTER THREE

WHAT TRUE LOVE IS

WE HAVE BEEN COMMANDED by our Creator not only to love Him but to love all the people He has created. Our Lord Jesus tells us that we must love each of them sacrificially, the way He loved us. So then, how, exactly, are we to define *love*?

This is not an easy question to answer in today's world. In fact, the Merriam Webster Dictionary gives nine separate meanings for the word *love*. These definitions range from a term for profoundly deep emotions to scoring zero points in a tennis match! We, ourselves, commonly use the word love to express everything from the enjoyment of an inanimate object to our deepest and most heartfelt feelings for someone we intensely cherish. For example, we say, "I love *pancakes*" just as easily as we say, "I love *you*." Not only is love one of the most commonly used and misused words in our vocabulary, regrettably, it is also a word that is frequently tossed about with careless insincerity and less than honorable intentions.

Given its multiple definitions and often inappropriate use, it is little wonder that we have been trying to define what true love is since our earliest recorded history. Millions of pieces of literature have been written, songs sung, music composed, and works of art created to describe, define, and capture the essence of love. Today, if we enter the word "love" into a search engine on the internet there are more than ten billion (yes, billion!) results referenced. These links direct us to everything from books to blogs, and their authors range from Ph.D.'s to poets, romantics to religious scholars, and countless people like you and me. We not only seem to be a world looking for love, but a world endlessly trying to define what true love is.

As Christians, however, you and I know that there is only one absolute expert who can define true love with perfect detail, unsurpassed knowledge, and unparalleled wisdom. There is quite literally nothing He does not know about love. He, too, has authored a book on love – a book so comprehensive that there is not a single characteristic of love that isn't covered. The entire book is, in and of itself, an example of the most incomparable love any of us will ever know. This compelling and inspirational book is, of course, the Holy Bible. From beginning to end the Bible encompasses every aspect of love: defines it, portrays it, explains it, and provides countless examples of it. It is the ultimate authority on love, divinely inspired by the very creator of love – God Himself. Who could define what true love is more beautifully, accurately, and correctly than the Author and Father of love, the God who *is* love? And what better guide could we possibly have than His personal instruction manual?

In His Holy Word, our Lord graciously teaches us everything we need to know about love: what it is, how to share it, and how critically important it is in the life of every person on earth. Not only does God teach us what love is, He richly and comprehensively helps us understand how to appropriately identify, develop, and experience the various kinds of love relationships He designed and created us to enjoy.

The love relationships described in the Bible fall into one of four primary categories. These categories are often identified by their Greek names: storge, philia, eros, and agape.

Storge is the natural or instinctive love and affection that family members, (parents, children, grandchildren, etc.) have for one another.

Philia is the brotherly or sisterly love between friends, a shared fondness and affectionate regard for one another. Philia is the root word in Philadelphia, which, as you may know, is commonly referred to as the "city of brotherly love."

Eros is the erotic or sensual aspect of love affiliated with sexual desire. By God's divine design eros is to be a sacred love experienced solely within the marital relationship between a husband and wife for emotional and psychological bonding, mutual physical pleasure, and procreation. Outside of this sacred unity eros is merely base desire or lust, which falls far short of the deep and fulfilling emotional, spiritual, and physical intimacy it was designed to be by our loving heavenly Father.

Agape (pronounced ag-ah'-pay) is charitable, or sacrificial, love; and it is the highest form of love. Agape is the kind of love our Lord Jesus was referring to when He commanded: "as I have loved you, so you must love one another." Through His perfect example, our Savior teaches us that agape selflessly seeks the highest good for others and is willing to pay the ultimate price to do so – even if that means sacrificing one's life to save another's. As such, agape is love in its purest, strongest, deepest, and most complete sense. It is the very height, depth, and breadth of what true love is.

Because of its unselfish and costly nature, agape requires a great deal more than tender feelings, empathy, or a compassionate heart for people. It requires us to make a conscious, deliberate (willful) choice to do good for others, including those whom we may feel are undeserving of it, regardless of the cost to ourselves. Agape, then, is intentional love put into action through service and sacrifice solely for the good of someone else.

With his beautifully poetic and inspiring definition, the apostle Paul helps us better understand true (agape) love by providing 15 specific characteristics of it. Seven of these characteristics are positive (what love is) while eight of them are negative (what love is not). Paul writes, "Love is patient, love is kind. It does not envy, it does not boast, it is not proud. It does not dishonor others, it is not self-seeking, it is not easily angered, it keeps no record of wrongs. Love does not delight in evil but rejoices with the truth. It always protects, always trusts, always hopes, always perseveres. Love never fails" (1 Corinthians 13:4-8).

Exploring each of these individual characteristics will help us better understand how each of us can put true (agape) love into practice as we endeavor to obey our Savior's commandment to love others the way He loved us.

LOVE IS PATIENT

Patience, as is often said, seems to be in short supply – especially in this fast-paced, me-first, got-to-have-it-now world where immediate gratification predominates our culture. In stark contrast, however, the apostle Paul tells us that to demonstrate true love patience must always prevail. Being patient means that we are willing to wait, as long as necessary, without grumbling, complaining, trying to hurry things up, or force things along. It means we remain calm when confronted with pressures, frustrations, offenses, and provocations; and that we display kindness, gentleness, dignity, and grace rather than outrage, anger, irritation, or resentment.

In practical, everyday experience it means waiting calmly in line to make a purchase, graciously smiling when someone cuts in front of us, and allowing them to go ahead of us even if we're in a hurry. It means not muttering ugly words under our breath when someone irritates or frustrates us or honking the horn at the driver in front of us the moment the stoplight turns green. It means keeping our cool when we've had a long, stressful day – even when we come home to an ill-tempered spouse, a moody teenager, or an inconsiderate roommate.

Patience is essential to our Christian witness because when we are patient, especially over long periods of time, we may be able to draw even the most obstinate and difficult people toward Christ Jesus. If we are willing to put forth the effort to wait, our patience, in combination with consistent loving kindness, can, over time, soften the sourest dispositions, reach those who seem unreachable, and overcome even the most hard-hearted of human beings.

There is no more perfect example of patience than God's patience with us. The apostle Peter reminds us, "Do not forget this one thing, dear friends: With the Lord a day is like a thousand years, and a thousand years are like a day. The Lord is not slow in keeping his promise, as some understand slowness. Instead he is patient with you, not wanting anyone to perish, but everyone to come to repentance … Bear in mind that our Lord's patience means salvation" (2 Peter 3:8-9, 15). God's patient love waits for us to come to him, to repent of our sins, and to give our lives to Christ Jesus. He then continues to demonstrate patient love for us as we struggle to stay faithful and obedient to Him yet continue to sin over and again.

Just as God's love for all of us is patient, we must, in turn, demonstrate patient love toward others, trusting that God is working all things out according to His perfect timing both in our lives and in the lives of others.

LOVE IS KIND

Patience and kindness go hand-in-hand because a kind person is patient and a patient person is kind. Being kind also means that with a tender, compassionate heart, a gentle, encouraging voice, and a loving spirit we look for tangible ways to care for people and make their lives better. It means continuously looking for ways to be helpful, encouraging, gracious, considerate, and thoughtful while actively trying to meet the physical, emotional, and spiritual needs of the people we encounter in our daily lives.

God continually demonstrates the kindness of His love for all people, both believers, and unbelievers, in countless ways every day. Jesus, speaking of His heavenly Father, tells us, "He makes his sun rise on the evil and the good, and sends rain on the just and on the unjust" (Matthew 5:45 NKJV). Not only does God provide sunshine and rain, food and clothing, family and friends, love and joy, but He also provides a way for all people to receive the forgiveness of their sins and the gift of eternal life. The apostle Paul reminds us, "[God] is so rich in kindness and grace that he purchased our freedom with the blood of his Son and forgave our sins" (Ephesians 1:7 NLT, emphasis mine).

Demonstrating loving-kindness to all people is not only an acknowledgment of our gratitude to God for His kindness to us, but it is also a demonstration of our commitment to follow the example Jesus set for us.

LOVE DOES NOT ENVY (IS NOT JEALOUS)

The apostle Paul makes this ardent appeal to all believers: "Let us not become conceited, or provoke one another, or be jealous of one another" (Galatians 5:26 NLT). To envy is to desire, or crave, something that belongs to someone else. Not only does envy drive us to take what isn't ours, it callously disregards and frequently harms the person who has what we want. James, the brother of Jesus, asks some pointed questions: "What is causing the quarrels and fights among you? Don't they come from the evil desires at war within you? You want what you don't have, so you scheme and kill to get it. You are jealous of what others have, but you can't get it, so you fight and wage war to take it away from them. Yet you don't have what you want because you don't ask God for it" (James 4:1-2 NLT).

Envy and jealousy are not only completely counter to the unselfish giving that is characteristic of true love, but they can, and often do, lead us directly into sin. James warns, "If you are bitterly jealous and there is selfish ambition in your heart, don't cover up the truth with boasting and lying. For jealousy and selfishness are not God's kind of wisdom. Such things are earthly, unspiritual, and demonic. For wherever there is jealousy and selfish ambition, there you will find disorder and evil of every kind" (James 3:14-16 NLT).

Envy is one of Satan's favorite tools. He used it in the garden of Eden to tempt Adam and Eve into taking the forbidden fruit, telling them if they ate it they would "be like God" (Genesis 3:5). Satan's words caused Adam and Eve to envy, or covet, God's superior wisdom and knowledge. That enviousness caused within them a corrupt desire to possess something that God had not given to them. Acting on those feelings led Adam and Eve to disobey God, commit the first sin, and cause the subsequent fall of all humankind. From that moment forward envy has been at the root of countless sins. Cain jealously slew his brother Abel; Joseph's envious brothers sold him into slavery; Daniel's jealous colleagues had him thrown into the lion's den, and so it goes right on up to us today. Envy and jealousy continue to bring out the worst in us as human beings and are entirely counter to the selflessness of true (agape) love.

As Christians, envy conveys to others not only a lack of love, but also a distinct lack of trust that God is both willing and able to provide well for us and meet all our needs. As such, instead of behaving jealously or envying others, we should lovingly (without resentment) delight in the blessings and gifts God has bestowed upon them. We should graciously celebrate other's accomplishments and successes, and trust that God, in His unfailing love and wisdom, will provide what He knows is best for each of us.

LOVE DOES NOT BOAST

King David reminds us, "The earth is the Lord's, and everything in it, the world, and all who live in it" (Psalm 24:1). Our loving and gracious God is the ultimate provider of everything we possess. Consequently, when we boast about ourselves – what we've accomplished, achieved, or acquired – we are placing ourselves ahead of Him, and taking credit for His gracious blessings and provisions in our lives.

Not only does God bless and provide for each of us, He sovereignly determines whether He will continue to bless us, bestow new blessings upon us, or take them all away. We can make all the plans we like and attempt to take credit for what we have, but God can change it all in a single heartbeat. King Solomon wisely advises, "Do not boast about tomorrow, for you do not know what a day may bring forth" (Proverbs 27:1 NKJV). Jesus' brother, James, admonishes, "Look here, you who say, 'Today or tomorrow we are going to a certain town and will stay there a year. We will do business there and make a profit.' How do you know what your life will be like tomorrow? Your life is like the morning fog – it's here a little while, then it's gone. What you ought to say is, 'If the Lord wants us to, we will live and do this or that.' Otherwise you are boasting about your own plans, and all such boasting is evil" (James 4:13-16 NLT).

Boasting is evil because when we engage in it, we tend to forget who we are, that we were all created by God, and we are all equal in His sight. We all live and breathe by His authority alone, and we are all sinners saved by His grace. When we take this fully into our hearts, there is no room for boasting – only for thanking and praising God that He loved us enough to save us and that He continues to bless and provide for us each day.

LOVE IS NOT PROUD

In the command to love as Jesus loved, our Lord commissions us to be humble, as He is, and put the good of others ahead of our own. The apostle Paul tells us, "Do nothing out of selfish ambition or vain conceit. Rather, in humility value others above yourselves" (Philippians 2:3).

Our Lord Jesus demonstrated total and complete humility. Although He was God, He became a servant to all humankind by taking the form of a Man, living in a broken world, and suffering deep humiliation and death for sinful people. The apostle Paul writes, "Though he was God,

[Jesus] did not think of equality with God as something to cling to. Instead, he gave up his divine privileges; he took the humble position of a slave and was born as a human being. When he appeared in human form, he humbled himself in obedience to God and died a criminal's death on a cross" (Philippians 2:6-8 NLT, emphasis mine).

Although Jesus modeled the way for us, total humility is an incredibly difficult concept for us to grasp. It just isn't in our nature to be humble. We inherently want to be important, recognized, and commended. Even Jesus' disciples struggled with pride. The apostle Paul's dear friend, the physician-evangelist, Luke, recalls, "[Jesus'] disciples began arguing about which of them was the greatest. But Jesus knew their thoughts, so he brought a little child to his side. Then he said to them, 'Anyone who welcomes a little child like this on my behalf welcomes me, and anyone who welcomes me also welcomes my Father who sent me. Whoever is the least among you is the greatest'" (Luke 9:46-48 NLT, emphasis mine).

King Solomon assures us, "When pride comes, then comes disgrace, but with humility comes wisdom" (Proverbs 11:2). Growing in the knowledge and wisdom of our Lord and Savior increases our desire to live humbly and obediently. Becoming more worldly, on the other hand, tends to lead us directly into self-centered pridefulness and sin. True charitable love keeps God first and keeps our own lives and the lives of others in their proper perspectives.

LOVE DOES NOT DISHONOR OTHERS

If kindness is one of the key attributes of love, as we have established it to be, then it stands to reason that offending someone with inappropriate words, gestures, actions, or conduct would be exceedingly unkind and therefore, also exceedingly unloving. True love, then, does not exhibit offensive, indecent, or shameful behavior. Instead, it is respectful and honorable. It demonstrates true Christlike character, behaving with dignity, sensitivity, grace, and integrity, and displaying thoughtful and considerate regard for others. Displaying good manners (saying please, thank you, excuse me, etc.); displaying good taste (avoiding any form of offensive conduct, inappropriate dress, vulgarity, or callousness); and maintaining a demeanor that honors and glorifies God are all essential components of true love.

Jesus never treated others unkindly, impolitely, arrogantly, or offensively. He never lashed out hatefully or berated others, even when they treated Him in the most appalling, disgraceful, and hurtful manner. For example, when Jesus' disciple and close friend, Judas Iscariot, betrays Him with a kiss in the garden of Gethsemane, our Lord calmly responds, "My friend, go ahead and do what you have come for" (Matthew 26:50 NLT). Later that same night in a legal proceeding Jesus stood before people who were viciously telling lies and giving false testimony about Him; yet, even then, He didn't retaliate, get angry, or even try to defend Himself against their fabricated accusations. He simply remained calm, composed, and quiet. Jesus' disciple, Matthew, describing this event tells us, "When [Jesus] was accused by the chief priests and the elders, he gave no answer. Then Pilate asked him, 'Don't you hear the testimony they are bringing against you?' But Jesus made no reply, not even to a single charge – to the great amazement of the governor" (Matthew 27:12-14, *emphasis mine*). In light of this, the apostle Peter reminds us, "For God called you to do good, even if it means suffering, just as Christ suffered for you. He is your example, and you must follow in his steps … He did not retaliate when he was insulted, nor threaten revenge when he suffered. He left his case in the hands of God, who always judges fairly" (1 Peter 2:21, 23 NLT).

Our Lord consistently demonstrated that regardless of the circumstances or situation we may find ourselves in, true love always displays selflessness, graciousness, honor, integrity, and respect for others as it steadfastly trusts that God is still ultimately in control. True love, therefore, always reflects Godly character.

LOVE IS NOT SELF-SEEKING

True love is not selfish, self-centered, self-indulgent, self-righteous, or self-seeking. It simply is not about *self*. It is precisely the opposite because, as we previously established, true (agape) love is selfless, always given without the desire for personal gain. Our Lord and Savior exemplified sacrificial, servant love – love that was selfless rather than self-centered, giving rather than greedy, and gracious and generous rather than self-gratifying. Jesus always focused outward, ever conscious of others' needs, willing to do whatever was necessary, even to the point of sacrificing His life to save us.

As Jesus' ambassadors and the image-bearers of God's love here on earth, we, too, must strive to develop an unselfish servant's heart, loving and caring for others even when it means making sacrifices. "Let each of you look out not only for his own interests, but also for the interests of others," instructs the apostle Paul (Philippians 2:4 NKJV). We must give of ourselves to others without holding back or expecting to get something in return. The physician-evangelist, Luke, reminds us, "You should remember the words of the Lord Jesus: 'It is more blessed to give than to receive'" (Acts 20:35 NLT).

LOVE IS NOT EASILY ANGERED

There are times when we all become angry, occasionally with intense passion over a cause we feel is just. Anger, in and of itself, is not a sin; it is a natural God-given emotion. We are each created with the ability to feel as well as, express anger.

Both our heavenly Father and our Lord and Savior, at times, expressed anger. Exodus Chapter Four tells us how Moses made excuses to God, attempting to explain why he wasn't the right person to approach Pharaoh and lead the Israelites out of Egypt. Moses' insolence finally goes too far, and we read in verse 14, "Then the Lord's anger burned against Moses" (Exodus 4:14). God was burning mad – so angry, in fact, that He considered, at one point, striking Moses dead! (Exodus 4:24) Even so, God was merciful and did not act harshly against Moses. Instead, with patience, compassion, tolerance, and wisdom He continued to work with Moses to come up with a plan Moses felt he could implement.

Jesus, too, displayed righteous anger when people were using the synagogue, His Father's house of worship, as a marketplace to conduct business and make money. The apostle John recalls, "When it was almost time for the Jewish Passover, Jesus went up to Jerusalem. In the temple courts he found people selling cattle, sheep and doves, and others sitting at tables exchanging money. So he made a whip out of cords, and drove all from the temple courts, both sheep and cattle; he scattered the coins of the money changers and overturned their tables. To those who sold doves he said, 'Get these out of here! Stop turning my Father's house into a market!'" (John 2:13-16) Our Lord was rightfully furious at such wicked and appalling behavior!

We are not precluded from expressing *just* or *righteous* anger, such as when an offense is committed against God or His Word, or in defense of someone who is being falsely accused or egregiously harmed. However, our anger should only be expressed within appropriate boundaries so that, as Christians, our loving, Christlike character is never compromised. This means we are never to act harshly, rashly, violently, create fear in others, or cause emotional or physical harm to anyone. James, Jesus' brother, wisely states, "Understand this, my dear brothers and sisters: You must all be quick to listen, slow to speak, and slow to get angry. Human anger does not produce the righteousness God desires" (James 1:19-20 NLT).

Inappropriate expressions of anger: being irrational, ill-tempered, enraged, or hateful over personal affronts, (especially if they stem from pride or selfishness), are not only unloving and unkind, they are sin. With this in mind, the apostle Paul warns, "Get rid of all bitterness, rage and anger, brawling and slander, along with every form of malice" (Ephesians 4:31). We must be very careful not to let our anger lead us into sin.

Given even the smallest foothold, Satan will try to use our anger against us by encouraging unforgiveness, retribution, retaliation, or in other ways cause hurt or harm to those who have irritated, offended, or injured us. When that kind of anger is allowed to grow and fester it always leads us directly into sin; and it often leaves utter devastation in its wake. Like a ticking bomb, uncontrolled anger will eventually cause us to blow up; and the damage left behind may be irreparable, devastating not only other's lives but ours as well. Consequently, we must never give Satan even the slightest opportunity to use anger to lead us into sin. My grandfather once shared with me these words of wisdom from the apostle Paul: "'Don't sin by letting anger control you.' Don't let the sun go down while you are still angry, for anger gives a foothold to the devil" (Ephesians 4:26-27 NLT). It is timeless, good advice!

When we stand firm in the grace and love of God, trusting that He will both judge and discipline the wrongs committed by all people, it allows us to let go of our anger and, instead, exercise the kind of charitable love Jesus places within our hearts.

LOVE KEEPS NO RECORD OF WRONGS

True, charitable, love does not bear grudges; nor does it dwell on past mistakes, insults, injuries, or injustices. Instead, it forgives and forgets all wrongs. Without question, this is one of the most challenging things for us to do. Consequently, it is helpful for us to remember that this is what God continually does for us. Our heavenly Father told the prophet, Jeremiah, that when His children repent: "I will forgive their wickedness and *will remember their sins no more*" (Jeremiah 31:34, emphasis mine). God chooses not to "remember" our sins from the moment we repent and ask Him for forgiveness. King David writes, "Blessed is the one whose transgressions are forgiven, whose sins are covered. *Blessed is the one whose sin the Lord does not count against them*" (Psalm 32:1-2, emphasis mine). God sees our human failures, flaws, missteps, and mistakes; yet, He continues to love us and gives us chance after chance to mend our ways. And when we ask for forgiveness, our Lord graciously wipes our slate clean.

If God, in His gracious love for us, does not keep a record of our entire lifetime's worth of sins but wipes our slate clean when we ask for His forgiveness, we must be willing to do the same when others have wronged us or someone for whom we care. We must continually try to see the good in others and overlook their shortcomings, wisely remembering that there are no perfect people, only imperfect people struggling to live in an imperfect world. King Solomon reminds us, "A person's wisdom yields patience; it is to one's glory to overlook an offense" (Proverbs 19:11).

In most instances, we are best served to let go of other's offenses. However, when someone does exhibit a behavior or error that is so significant it must be addressed, we should do so privately with a gentle, respectful, and loving approach; and then let the matter go completely. We must never keep a list (mentally or otherwise) of offenses or wrongs nor harbor resentment against anyone. It is also important to remember that we cannot build one another up or help someone grow in God's grace if we keep beating them back down.

LOVE DOES NOT DELIGHT IN EVIL, BUT REJOICES WITH THE TRUTH

True love takes no pleasure in anything that causes hurt or harm to any person (including ourselves). It finds no joy in our own or others' evil actions, immorality, violence, vulgarity, nor in the sensationalizing of evil or sin in any form (including television programs, movies, books, magazines, digital entertainment, broadcast, or other media). Genuine love finds no delight in telling lies, repeating gossip, speaking falsely, disparaging someone, or damaging anyone's reputation. Rather, true love graciously shares the truth of God's Word and rejoices when others live according to the laws of His love.

Especially in our world today, where the ugliness of sin and evil surround us at every turn, we must always try to do what is right and good and hold fast to the Word of God as our guide for living life in this broken and sinful world. The author of Psalm 97 instructs, "Let those who love the Lord hate evil, for he guards the lives of his faithful ones and delivers them from the hand of the wicked" (Psalm 97:10). The prophet Amos tells us plainly, "Hate evil; love good" (Amos 5:15 NKJV).

The only way for us to hate evil and love good is to have a clear understanding of what good and evil are according to the truth of God's Word. Yet, regrettably, many people, including some self-professing Christians, no longer believe in the whole truth of God's Word, nor see it as the only absolute truth.

Sadly, many people today think there is no absolute truth, accepting instead that truth is whatever each person wants it to be. Additionally, we are taught that to be "politically correct" we must be tolerant and accepting of all peoples' beliefs, behaviors, personal values, and morality as equally valid and acceptable. As such, we are experiencing ever-increasing pressure to embrace all ideologies rather than remaining faithfully committed to the inerrant truth of God's Word.

In this tolerant twenty-first century, holding fast to God's Word as the only absolute truth and not allowing false teachers and/or teachings to go unchecked (even when we do so with the utmost care, respect, and love) is bringing increased persecution and condemnation to many faithful Christians in the United States and around the world. Here in America our religious freedom and the right to live out our Christian faith are being threatened as never before. And sadly, as I am writing this, thousands of Christians in parts of the Middle East, China, North Korea, and Africa are in hiding or fleeing for their lives. Others are being tortured and put to death by crucifixion, burning, beheading, and other horrific methods because they refuse to disavow their Savior and the truth of God's Word.

We can expect that the persecution of Christians all over the world will only continue to increase as time goes on. This makes it even more essential for us, as the followers of Christ Jesus, to faithfully proclaim the Truth, defend the Truth, and work diligently to see that the whole truth of God's Word is accurately upheld and maintained. The apostle Paul advises, "Do your best to present yourself to God as one approved, a worker who does not need to be ashamed and who correctly handles the word of truth" (2 Timothy 2:15). No matter the consequences, we must always seek good over evil, and never compromise when it comes to the truth of God's Word.

LOVE ALWAYS PROTECTS

True love, with God's help, stands up under (bears) the weight of others' weaknesses and mistakes. It understands that human beings are fragile, flawed, and far from perfect. Authentic love covers people's shortcomings, inadequacies, and failures with a shield of privacy, and desires that the dignity of all people is safeguarded. Love, therefore, graciously shelters people from harm; and it never exposes anyone to embarrassment, ridicule, gossip, or derision.

Without question, it can be very challenging to protect others and place a shield of grace over them – particularly when we find ourselves in the uncomfortable position of having been taken advantage of or mistreated by someone. At such times, our initial desire is more likely to disgrace them than to protect them graciously. For this reason, keeping Christlike love at the forefront of our thoughts is essential if we want to avoid embarking on a course of action we will later regret. Especially today, in the age of instant messaging and real-time social media, we must exercise extreme caution, or we can easily find ourselves going down an ungodly path in a matter of seconds. While we are never to tolerate, condone, ignore, or approve of sinful behavior, we must never expose anyone to harm for their mistakes (publicly or privately).

True love is also a champion and protector of the poor, the weak, and the disadvantaged. We must, as King Solomon teaches, "Speak up for those who cannot speak for themselves, for the rights of all who are destitute. Speak up and judge fairly; defend the rights of the poor and needy" (Proverbs 31:8-9). Just as Jesus continually championed the poor, the sick, the marginalized, and the oppressed so we also must protect and defend them and in tangible, loving ways seek what is right and helpful for all people according to God's Word.

LOVE ALWAYS TRUSTS

True love is eager to believe the best in people, focus on the good in others, and trust that they are honorable, upright, and honest. It is willing to give people the benefit of the doubt in questionable situations, consider their circumstances, and not lose sight of their positive qualities amid their faults or failures. We all make mistakes and have character flaws, but charitable love looks past them to see the basic good in people to the greatest extent possible.

Many people think this verse requires that we blindly trust everyone and believe everything people say. However, this is not the case because love and trust are not at odds with wisdom and discernment. King Solomon tells us, "The simple believe anything, but the prudent give thought to their steps" (Proverbs 14:15).

When we have trusted someone and then receive irrefutable proof that they are not worthy of our trust or belief in them, we must be prudent and cautious in our dealings with that person. We will need to remain vigilant, and possibly terminate or suspend our interactions with them, at least until they prove themselves worthy of our trust once again.

It is likely that all of us will experience a violation of our trust at some point in time. That breach, however, should never prevent us from reaching out to others with love and trust in the future. Whatever the outcome of our interactions with others, we are always assured of one thing: God's hand is at work in our lives, He is molding and shaping us into the image of His Son, and we can count on Him to see us through every situation with the promise of one day joining Him for all eternity. "Don't let your hearts be troubled," instructs our Lord Jesus. "Trust in God, and trust also in me" (John 14:1 NLT).

LOVE ALWAYS HOPES

There is a compelling poem titled "Lend Me Your Hope" that beautifully expresses what so many of us feel when hopelessness descends upon us. The unknown author wrote:

> *Lend me your hope for a while,*
> *I seem to have mislaid mine.*
> *Lost and hopeless feelings accompany me daily,*
> *pain and confusion are my companions.*
> *I know not where to turn.*
> *Looking ahead to future times*
> *does not bring forth images of renewed hope.*
> *I see troubled times,*
> *pain-filled days,*
> *and more tragedy.*
> *Lend me your hope for a while,*
> *I seem to have mislaid mine.*
> *Hold my hand and hug me;*
> *listen to all my ramblings,*
> *recovery seems so far distant.*
> *The road to healing seems like a long and lonely one.*
> *Lend me your hope for a while,*
> *I seem to have mislaid mine.*
> *Stand by me,*
> *offer me your presence,*
> *your heart and your love.*

WHAT TRUE LOVE IS

Acknowledge my pain,
it is so real and ever present.
I am overwhelmed
with sad and conflicting thoughts.
Lend me your hope for a while.
A time will come when I will heal,
and I will share my renewal,
hope and love with others.

There are times in each of our lives when we feel hopeless, when the burdens and heartaches of life overwhelm us, and feelings of despair set in. Nevertheless, as the prophet Isaiah assures us, "Those who hope in the Lord will renew their strength. They will soar on wings like eagles; they will run and not grow weary, they will walk and not be faint" (Isaiah 40:31). Our loving Lord is always there to help, encourage, support, protect, guide, and teach us. "So, be strong and courageous, all you who put hope in the Lord!" encourages King David (Psalm 31:24 NLT).

As Christians, our faith in God's unfailing love for us and our trust in the finished work of Christ Jesus on our behalf are the reasons for our hope. We know that no matter how difficult the circumstances might be today or tomorrow, God is with us through them all; and we have His assurance there will be a brighter future ahead. This knowledge is what enables us to share the hope we have with others in a world filled with so much hopelessness, uncertainty, suffering, and fear, and pray with the psalmist: "Let your unfailing love surround us, Lord, for our hope is in you alone" (Psalm 33:22 NLT).

LOVE ALWAYS PERSEVERES

True love never quits, never tires, and never gives up regardless of the circumstances. It endures through disappointment, discouragement, heartache, suffering, sorrow, and grief. It is steadfast and unchanging in the face of persecution, oppression, and mistreatment. Genuine love refuses to yield to temptation, outlasts every assault our enemies (including Satan) bring against us, and stands steadfastly in the strength, goodness, and grace of God.

God declares through the prophet Jeremiah, "I have loved you with an *everlasting* love; I have drawn you with unfailing kindness" (Jeremiah 31:3, emphasis mine). God's everlasting love is love that perseveres – eternally. Even in the face of our sins and failures, the promise God made to Joshua remains true for us: "As I was with Moses, so I will be with you; I will never leave you nor forsake you" (Joshua 1:5). God has not and never will give up on loving and caring for us! We, in turn, should not give up on loving Him and sharing His love with others.

The apostle Paul prayed, "May the Lord direct your hearts into God's love and Christ's perseverance" (2 Thessalonians 3:5). When God's love fills our hearts, and Jesus' example is our motivation we, too, will be able to persevere, not giving up even when we face disappointment, discouragement, fear, heartache, or grief. Through the power of God's Spirit working within us true love can endure even when others disrespect, hurt, or mistreat us, and the temptation to withhold our love from them in return grows strong.

God will never let us down or leave us alone to face life's challenges or sorrows. He will always see us through and give us the strength to go on. His love will keep us going even when the going gets too rough for us to navigate on our own. With God's help, love will not only prevail but will gain a commanding victory over everything that comes our way. The Italian poet, Virgil, famously said, "Love conquers all things; let us too surrender to love."[3] When we surrender our hearts and submit our lives to the God who *is* love, Love does indeed conquer all!

---

[3] Publius Virgilius Maro, "Virgil" (70 BC – 19 BC), *Eclogues*

LOVE NEVER FAILS

While true love, with God's help, unfailingly conquers all, we can and do grow weary when we are suffering or hurt. At times, the pain is so great that we just want to give up. Human beings are broken, sinful, and fallible; therefore, we can and do let one another down, sometimes hurting each other beyond what we think we can endure. But God will always be there to comfort us, help us, encourage us, and restore us. As the psalmist, Asaph, expresses so poignantly, "My health may fail, and my spirit may grow weak, but God remains the strength of my heart; he is mine forever" (Psalm 73:26 NLT).

Human love may falter or fail, but God's love never will. He will never forsake or forget us. He will never turn His back on us. He will always be there for us no matter what happens. The psalmists ardently proclaim: "For the Lord is good and his love endures forever; his faithfulness continues through all generations ... Your love, Lord, reaches to the heavens, your faithfulness to the skies ... I trust in God's unfailing love for ever and ever" (Psalm 100:5; Psalm 36:5; Psalm 52:8). Because God's love is unfailing, we know that regardless of our own or others' failures here on earth, our heartaches, or the disasters that may befall us God's love can and will overcome them all. The author of Lamentations assures us, "Though [God] brings grief, he also shows compassion because of the greatness of his unfailing love" (Lamentations 3:32 NLT, emphasis mine).

Although, as Christian, we have God's promise of unfailing love, many of us are nevertheless afraid to love others with all our hearts. Perhaps we've been deeply hurt by someone or have experienced the heartbreaking loss of human love. While, in such circumstances, it may be exceedingly difficult, we must remember that there is no reason to be fearful because God will see us through anything and everything we might face. King David articulates this perfectly, proclaiming, "The Lord is my light and my salvation – whom shall I fear? The Lord is the stronghold of my life – of whom shall I be afraid?" (Psalm 27:1).

No matter what may happen in this broken, sinful world, as followers of Christ Jesus, our eternal destiny is secure. All our sins are forgiven. There will be no punishment or retribution. And as Jesus' beloved disciple, John, tells us, "There will be no more death or mourning or crying or pain" (Revelation 21:4). We will be wholly enveloped in our heavenly Father's loving presence. Therefore, we have absolutely nothing to fear in giving true love away without reservation. "There is no fear in love," explains John. "But perfect love drives out fear, because fear has to do with punishment. The one who fears is not made perfect in love" (1 John 4:18). Everyone who has accepted Jesus as their Savior has been "made perfect in love" – set free to love without fear because we are assured of God's unfailing love both here on earth and for all eternity.

Our Lord Jesus wants each one of us to live in His love, to love others as He loves us: with true charitable love – love that is patient, kind, gracious, humble, unselfish, amiable, forgiving, truthful, honorable, and faithful. And He wants us to do so freely, without fear, uncertainty, or doubt. Our Lord has assured us that we will never be without Him as we endeavor to obey the commandment to love others as He loved us.

A Word

"Show me your ways, Lord, teach me your paths. Guide me in your truth and teach me, for you are God my Savior, and my hope is in you all day long" (Psalm 25:4-5).

And A Prayer

"I pray that the eyes of your heart may be enlightened in order that you may know the hope to which he has called you, the riches of his glorious inheritance in his holy people, and his incomparably great power for us who believe" (Ephesians 1:18-19).

CHAPTER FOUR

LOVE WITH DIVINE HELP

MOST OF US FIND IT RELATIVELY EASY to show true charitable love to our family members and friends. We willingly care for them and try to meet their needs, often putting their needs ahead of our own. We show them kindness and affection, bear their shortcomings, forgive their mistakes, and otherwise demonstrate our love for them in a myriad of ways. We make sure they have enough food to eat, clothing to wear, and a safe place to sleep. We care for them when they're sick or injured. We comfort, support, and encourage them when they suffer heartaches, challenges, and difficulties. We protect and defend them. And we celebrate their successes and share in their joys. It is natural to love this way when we have an emotional attachment to another person.

However, as we know, our Lord's commandment to love and care for all people goes far beyond our family members and friends. So, how then, are we to love all the people we encounter in our lives: those we don't really know, or perhaps don't really like, or those with whom we have no relationship at all? It seems reasonable to wonder if it is even possible to love *all* people. How do we love complete strangers? How do we love those we find virtually unlovable? Many of us, if we are willing to admit it, have had the unfortunate experience of looking at another human being and thinking it would be virtually impossible to love that person. Can we truly love the person who is angry and hateful or the one who has greatly wronged us or someone we love? When we consider the evil, hurtful actions people engage in every day and the heinous crimes such as torture, rape, murder, and the unspeakable acts perpetrated upon innocent children, it seems doubtful we could ever find it within ourselves to truly love *all* people.

Indeed, if we are completely honest, most of us find it challenging enough to show true charitable love to those we genuinely care for when they have hurt, offended, or wronged us or someone close to us. How much more difficult it would be, then, to love someone with whom we don't have an emotional connection who has committed an extremely egregious offense. Most of us would conclude that in our own strength it would be virtually impossible for us to love all people, especially those whose behavior we find utterly reprehensible or even abominable. Well, if we came to that conclusion, we would be correct. As imperfect, sinful human beings, none of us can demonstrate true charitable (agape) love toward all people, in all circumstances, on our own. Fortunately for us, we have God's help; and our Lord and Savior assures us that "with God all things are possible" (Matthew 19:26 NKJV).

God, in His great love and wisdom, has provided us with a powerful set of tools to help us express true charitable love toward all our neighbors – whoever they may be. He has given us the Bible, His own personal instruction manual; Jesus, His own Son, as the perfect example for us to follow; the Holy Spirit to live within us and be our constant guide, helper, and counselor; prayer to keep us in continual communication with Him; and the fellowship of other believers to support, strengthen, and encourage us. Through these resources, our Lord teaches us, equips us, and enables us to obey His command to demonstrate true charitable love toward all people.

Let's take a closer look at each of these extraordinary resources that God has so graciously and lovingly provided for us.

GOD'S WORD

The Holy Bible is God's love letter to His entire creation, to all people in all the world. Through divine inspiration and authority our Creator reveals His character, His attitudes, His expectations, His laws, His sovereign power, might, and wisdom, His blessings, the extraordinary depth of His unfailing, unconditional, saving love for us, and His will for our lives as His beloved creation.

The Bible teaches us how we are to love God; worship, praise, and thank Him; and how we are to give glory and honor to Him in return for all He has done for us. It teaches us how to live here on earth, remain faithful, be fruitful and productive, and fulfill God's intended purpose for our lives. It is the ultimate guidebook to know true love and have abundant life – here on earth and for eternity. Jesus reminds us, "Man shall not live on bread alone, but on every word that comes from the mouth of God" (Matthew 4:4).

The Bible is full of God's wisdom, advice, and direction along with vivid examples and illustrations that teach us how best to live and love in this sinful, broken world. It helps us get through the trials we face, guides us in the choices we make, and tells us how to receive our Lord's greatest blessings. "All Scripture is inspired by God and is useful to teach us what is true and to make us realize what is wrong in our lives. It corrects us when we are wrong and teaches us to do what is right. God uses it to prepare and equip his people to do every good work," explains the apostle Paul. (2 Timothy 3:16-17 NLT).

God divinely inspired the writers of Scripture to employ a variety of different genres as they recorded His Word to make it informative, interesting, diverse, understandable, relevant, and enjoyable. The original authors utilized personal stories, historical accounts, hyperbole, prose, poetry, parables, and songs. Although they wrote in the language of their respective cultures and times, they wrote only what God divinely inspired them to write. It was this divine inspiration that made the original writings of Scripture the inerrant Word of God.

Since the original words of the Bible have been spiritually written, only those believers who have the Holy Spirit living and working within them can accurately understand and apply the Word of God. The apostle Paul tells us, "We have received God's Spirit (not the world's spirit), so we can know the wonderful things God has freely given us. When we tell you these things, we do not use words that come from human wisdom. Instead, we speak words given to us by the Spirit, using the Spirit's words to explain spiritual truths. But people who aren't spiritual can't receive these truths from God's Spirit. It all sounds foolish to them and they can't understand it, for only those who are spiritual can understand what the Spirit means" (1 Corinthians 2:12-14 NLT).

As God's children, blessed to have His Spirit within us, we must be faithful and diligent in studying His Word. The apostle Paul reminds us, "Everything that was written in the past was written to teach us, so that through the endurance taught in the Scriptures and the encouragement they provide we might have hope" (Romans 15:4). Scripture, God's precious and holy Word, is an extraordinarily rich resource and the ultimate instruction manual for living Christlike lives. We must not only read and study it, but we must also continually apply it in our daily lives. As James, our Lord's brother, instructs, "Do not merely listen to the word, and so deceive yourselves. *Do what it says*" (James 1:22, emphasis mine).

We will always gain the most significant knowledge and wisdom of God, His Word, and His will for our lives by studying the Bible as a whole. To that end, I encourage you to search out God's Word in its entirety. The richness and depth of love and guidance you will find there will, without question, be of great help to you and bless your life immeasurably.

JESUS' EXAMPLE

One of the best ways for us to do what Scripture says is to follow the example set for us by our Lord and Savior, Jesus Christ. However, for us to follow Jesus' example, to truly emulate Him in our lives, we must first get to know Him on a deeply personal level – not just know *about* Him but know Him intimately. The apostle Peter tells us, "By his divine power, God has given us everything we need for living a godly life. We have received all of this by coming to know [Jesus], the one who called us to himself by means of his marvelous glory and excellence. And because of his glory and excellence, he has given us great and precious promises. These are the promises that enable you to share his divine nature and escape the world's corruption caused by human desires. In view of all this, make every effort to respond to God's promises. Supplement your faith with a generous provision of moral excellence, and moral excellence with knowledge, and knowledge with self-control, and self-control with patient endurance, and patient endurance with godliness, and godliness with brotherly affection with love for everyone. *The more you grow like this, the more productive and useful you will be in your knowledge of our Lord Jesus Christ*" (2 Peter 1:3-8 NLT, emphasis mine).

Once we have diligently sought to know who Jesus is and allowed His teachings to permeate our hearts and minds, we will be able to begin incorporating into our own lives the very characteristics our Lord Jesus Himself embodied.

The author of Hebrews said of Jesus: "The Son is the radiance of God's glory and the exact representation of his being" (Hebrews 1:3). Jesus, being one with God, demonstrated all the characteristics of God's perfect love and holiness. However, He was also fully human. Our Lord felt hunger, thirst, weariness, and temptation. He was a son, brother, and friend. He laughed and cried, felt righteous anger, and experienced deep humiliation and excruciating pain. Our Savior knew all the pain as well as the joys of life on earth; and that knowledge made Him the most understanding, compassionate, and loving Man who ever lived.

Despite the unbearable burden He carried for humanity, Jesus overflowed with love, radiated genuine joy, and projected perfect peace. He was warm, welcoming, open, cheerful, and friendly. I'm sure no one could light up a room as our Lord did! He was engaging and enthusiastic with an impressive, expressive, and irresistibly magnetic personality. At the same time, our Savior exuded holiness and authority, conducting Himself with both honor and humility. Even when Jesus performed miracles, He did them humbly, quietly, and calmly without fanfare, drama, or showy exhibitions, sometimes telling those He healed not to tell anyone what He had done for them. (Matthew 8:4; Mark 7:36.) When we look for role models in this broken, self-centered, media-driven world Jesus' life stands markedly apart; and He alone is the one we should be striving to emulate.

Our Lord and Savior lived life fully during His time on earth. And while He often took quiet personal time alone to meditate and pray, He was also a social person who spent a good deal of time in the public eye. He attended dinners, holiday events, and weddings; and He often addressed large gatherings. Regardless of the venue, Jesus was always a true gentleman: honorable, respectful, well-mannered, gracious, kind, and patient. He was ready and willing to talk with anyone and everyone: family, friends, strangers, and even His enemies. He was strong, steadfast, and filled with conviction; He was also gentle, compassionate, and caring, always ready and eager to help; and tireless in His desire to share God's love with everyone He encountered.

Jesus evoked feelings of confidence, safety, and trustworthiness in those He met. We know this because even little children readily came to Him. Young children have a strong inner sense about people, intuitively discerning who is safe to approach and who they need to shy away from or even fear. Parents, also, are always on alert and protective of their children. The apostle Mark recalls, "One day some parents brought their children to Jesus so he could touch and bless them ... Then he took the children in his arms and placed his hands on their heads and blessed them" (Mark 10:13, 16 NLT). Not only did the little children instinctively trust Jesus, but their naturally protective parents also did, or they would never have allowed their precious little ones to get so close to Him.

Jesus was humble, faithful, and obedient to His heavenly Father. He demonstrated the depth of His love, adoration, and obedience to God by loving all humanity with a love so unselfish that He gave up His rightful place in heaven, lived on earth as a Man for more than 30 years, and then sacrificed His life to save us before being raised to His heavenly throne once again. Jesus was, and is, the perfect example of true charitable (agape) love – an example He wants each of us to follow.

When Jesus said "follow me" to His first disciples, He meant more than for them to tag along and keep Him company as He traveled and taught. He meant for them to emulate Him in thought and spirit as well as in words and actions. Our Savior has the same requirement for us today. "*Whoever* wants to be my disciple," instructs Jesus, "must deny themselves and take up their cross and follow me" (Mark 8:34, emphasis mine). Following Jesus means that we must learn to let go of our old self-centered, worldly ways and strive to love others charitably and sacrificially, the way He loved us.

Faithfully following our Lord and Savior is not a part-time, half-hearted, only on Sundays, or when-we-feel-like-it endeavor. Jesus makes this clear when He reminds us of His Father's words to the prophet Isaiah concerning people who are not fully committed to Him or to obeying His Word, stating, "These people honor me with their lips, but their hearts are far from me" (Matthew 15:8). Jesus knows His true followers. He tells us plainly, "I know my sheep and my sheep know me – just as the Father knows me and I know the Father" (John 10:14-15).

The only way for us to be committed followers of Jesus and to live faithful, Christlike lives is to continually seek a deeper relationship with Him, study His teaching, stay in constant fellowship with Him, and follow the example He set for us. "Remain in me, and I also remain in you" directs Jesus. "No branch can bear fruit by itself; it must remain in the vine. Neither can you bear fruit unless you remain in me. I am the vine; you are the branches. If you remain in me and I in you, you will bear much fruit; apart from me you can do nothing ... This is to my Father's glory, that you bear much fruit, showing yourselves to be my disciples" (John 15:4-5, 8).

The more we read, study, and hear God's Word the more we will grow to understand, trust, and depend upon our Savior. The more we comprehend the depth of Jesus' love for us, the deeper our love for Him and our commitment to Him will grow. Eventually, the love relationship we have with Him will become the central focus of our lives, and we will no longer be able to contain the pure joy we experience in knowing Him. When we have such a deeply personal, intimate relationship with Christ Jesus, when His love virtually overflows our hearts, we will not only be ready to share His love with others it won't be possible for us to keep it to ourselves!

HELP FROM THE HOLY SPIRIT

God graciously ensures that every person who accepts Christ Jesus as their Savior will not only have His example to follow, but His Spirit within them to help, guide, and teach them. The Holy Spirit, Paraclete in Greek or Paracletus in Latin, means *advocate, or one who comes alongside to help*. Jesus said of Him: "I will ask the Father, and he will give you another advocate to help you and be with you forever – the Spirit of truth. The world cannot accept him, because it neither sees him nor knows him. But you know him, for *he lives with you and will be in you* ... The Advocate, the Holy Spirit, whom the Father will send in my name, will teach you all things and will remind you of everything I have said to you" (John 14:16-17, 26, emphasis mine).

Our Lord and Savior graciously sent the Holy Spirit to live within the hearts and minds of believers after His death because He knew we would need divine help and intervention to faithfully and obediently live the new life to which He calls us. As such, through the indwelling of the Holy Spirit, we have the power and advocacy of all three persons of the Trinity at work in our lives:

God the Father, our Creator – "For it is God who works in you to will and to act in order to fulfill his good purpose" (Philippians 2:13);

God the Son, Jesus our Savior – "You also were included in Christ when you heard the message of truth, the gospel of your salvation" (Ephesians 1:13); and

God the Holy Spirit – "When you believed, you were marked in [Christ] with a seal, the promised Holy Spirit, who is a deposit guaranteeing our inheritance until the redemption of those who are God's possession – to the praise of his glory" (Ephesians 1:13-14, emphasis mine).

The Holy Spirit living within us is a powerful force in our lives. He gives us strength, wisdom, understanding, and direction. He enables us to be humble and faithful and to fulfill God's commandments to love Him and others with commitment, confidence, and conviction. The apostle Paul states, "God has not given us a spirit of fear, but of power and of love and of a sound mind [self-discipline]" (2 Timothy 1:7 NKJV, emphasis mine).

The Holy Spirit's presence and work in our lives, combined with our willingness to be obedient to God, produces what the apostle Paul terms "the fruit of the Spirit," nine specific traits that our Lord Jesus Himself embodied. Paul tells us, "The fruit of the Spirit is love, joy, peace, forbearance, kindness, goodness, faithfulness, gentleness and self-control" (Galatians 5:22-23).

Notice that while Paul has given us nine characteristics, they collectively comprise the singular fruit of the Spirit. As such, when we invite Christ Jesus into our lives, submit our will to Him, and welcome the Holy Spirit into our hearts, He begins to produce within us all nine of these Christlike attributes. In this way, the fruit of the Spirit becomes the outward evidence that we are Jesus' faithful followers, indwelt by the Holy Spirit, and committed to our Heavenly Father.

Since the fruit of the Spirit is such an integral part of our lives as followers of Christ Jesus, let's take a closer look at each of these nine essential traits that comprise the fruit (working) of the Holy Spirit.

Love (Agape) – Love is the first and primary element of the fruit of the Spirit because, as we previously learned from the apostle John, God is love. Consequently, because God is love and we have been born anew in Him, having accepted Jesus as our Savior, we now possess through the power of the Holy Spirit, our Creator's loving nature. As the apostle Paul tells us, "God's love has been poured out into our hearts through the Holy Spirit, who has been given to us" (Romans 5:5). You and I possess the very love of God within us. As such, every time we demonstrate God's love to the world around us this powerful, life-changing fruit of the Spirit is revealed.

Joy – Genuine, spiritual joy is not the same thing as earthly happiness. Happiness is based upon our emotions and dictated by what we see, hear, feel, and perceive. In other words, our circumstances determine our happiness. Spiritual joy, however, is not dependent upon what happens *to* us, but on the knowledge of what our Lord and Savior has already done *for* us. Spiritual joy, therefore, is not based upon our situation or circumstances, but upon our relationship with Christ our Savior.

Jesus' joy is our perfect example. The author of Hebrews tells us, "For the joy set before him he endured the cross, scorning its shame, and sat down at the right hand of the throne of God" (Hebrews 12:2). On the face of it, it's hard to see how Jesus could have joy in His suffering on the cross or in the shame He endured before regaining His rightful place in heaven. But a closer look shows us that Jesus' joy is not based upon His circumstances or situation. It comes, instead, from the relationship He has with His loving heavenly Father and from carrying out His divine will. In carrying out His Father's will, our Lord knew He would be reunited with His Father in heaven, and through His sacrifice and suffering each of His beloved followers would be forgiven of their sins and join Him in heaven for eternity. Jesus' joy was, therefore, relational, that is based on His relationship as opposed to His situation or circumstances.

As you and I are led by the Holy Spirit to know and understand all that God has done for us through Jesus' sacrifice, we cannot help but be filled with sincere, heartfelt gratitude, humble acceptance, and irrepressible joy – joy that is not based upon our earthly circumstances, but on our relationship with God and His promise of eternal life. When this kind of spiritual joy fills our hearts through the working of the Holy Spirit it can't help but flow out of us and into the lives of people around us – brightening difficult days, softening hardened hearts, encouraging those in despair, and drawing people a little closer to the love of their Lord and Savior.

Peace – Jesus tells us, "Peace I leave with you; my peace I give you. I do not give to you as the world gives. Do not let your hearts be troubled and do not be afraid" (John 14:27). The peace our Savior has given to us through the working of the Holy Spirit not only frees us from worry and fear, it gives us a deep sense of well-being, confidence, and inner calm that stem from the assurance of His loving hand upon our lives, the knowledge that all His promises will come to fruition, and the certainty of eternal life in His presence.

As the peace of our Lord increasingly fills our hearts and minds, we will be better able to maintain a deep inner tranquility and develop more peaceable relationships with other people – even those with whom we may, at times, experience significant strife or conflict. King David reminds us that whatever we may encounter, we have this assurance: "The Lord will give strength to his people; the Lord will bless his people with peace" (Psalm 29:11 NKJV).

Patience – The Greek word for patience is *makrothumia* which means long-passion or long-tempered, which, of course, is the opposite of short-tempered and impatient. We are all too often easily exasperated, annoyed, and anxious – especially in this age of instant communication, instant information, and the continual desire for instant gratification.

Fortunately, when the Holy Spirit works within us, reminding us both of God's extraordinary patience with us and the peace we are blessed to have through our relationship with Christ Jesus, serenity and patience will grow within us. Then, as the Holy Spirit continues to help us trust in God's perfect timing (both in our lives and the lives of others), we will find it ever easier to "wait for the Lord; be strong and take heart and wait for the Lord" (Psalm 27:14).

Kindness – Throughout His life, Jesus exhibited kindness to everyone, even to those who treated Him deplorably. Our Savior was kind (helpful, considerate, caring, compassionate, and gracious) to every man, woman, and child He encountered. He was kind to the sick, handicapped, mentally ill, and demon possessed. He was kind to the Samaritans (who were hated enemies of the Jews). He was kind to those who rejected Him and the gospel message. He was kind to Judas, His betrayer. And He was kind to His tormentors, including the hateful Pharisees and Sadducees, the patronizing high priest, the corrupt governor who sentenced Him to death, the Roman soldiers who crucified Him, and the taunting thieves hanging next to Him on the cross.

Our Lord epitomized kindness; and His Spirit is now at work within us as His followers so that we, too, may extend genuine kindness to all people – our friends and enemies alike. Kindness can open even the hardest of hearts as we share the love of God and the gospel message with others through the working of the Holy Spirit within us.

Goodness – Jesus once told a wealthy young ruler: "No one is good – except God alone" (Luke 18:19). God is indeed good; and all of Scripture reflects His goodness, grace, mercy, and love as well as His justice and righteousness. King David, describing God's goodness, tells us, "The Lord is merciful and compassionate, slow to get angry and filled with unfailing love. The Lord is good to everyone. He showers compassion on all his creation … The Lord is good and does what is right; he shows the proper path to those who go astray. He leads the humble in doing right, teaching them his way … How great is the goodness you have stored up for those who fear you. You lavish it on those who come to you for protection, blessing them before the watching world" (Psalm 145:8-9; 25:8-9; 31:19 NLT).

We can see God's goodness in everything He created both on earth and in the heavens. James, Jesus' brother, acknowledges, "Every good and perfect gift is from above, coming down from the Father of the heavenly lights, who does not change like shifting shadows" (James 1:17). From the beginning of time God has continued to provide good gifts to all people: those who are saved (to bless us) and to the unsaved (so they can see His gracious kindness, turn away from sin, and give their hearts and lives to Him).

Our Lord graciously equips us, through His Holy Spirit, to demonstrate goodness toward others. The apostle Peter assures us, "[God's] divine power has given us everything we need for a godly life through our knowledge of [Jesus] who called us by his own glory and goodness" (2 Peter 1:3, emphasis mine).

Sharing and modeling the goodness of God through the power of the

Holy Spirit is key to overcoming the evil, sin, brokenness, and injustice in our present world and drawing people toward their Savior. We, therefore, pray with the apostle Paul: "May [God] give [us] the power to accomplish all the good things [our] faith prompts [us] to do" (2 Thessalonians 1:11 NLT, emphasis mine).

Faithfulness – "The Lord is trustworthy in all he promises and faithful in all he does. The Lord upholds all who fall and lifts up all who are bowed down … Your love, Lord, reaches to the heavens, your faithfulness to the skies," declares King David (Psalm 145:13-14; 36:5). Faithfulness means being trustworthy, steadfast, believable, loyal, devoted, and unfailingly true to one's word regardless of external influences or circumstances. Our heavenly Father is all these things and more. We can trust and count on His unchanging love for us and that He will keep every promise He has ever made to us without exception.

Jesus, ever our perfect role-model, demonstrated unrivaled faithfulness. He was faithful to God and proved to each of us that we could trust Him by obediently honoring His Father, fulfilling prophecy, and laying down His life for us.

Now our Savior has appointed and entrusted us to convey His faithfulness to the world and to serve as His ambassadors, sharing both His love and the gospel message. However, as the apostle Paul points out, "It is required that those who have been given a trust must prove faithful" (1 Corinthians 4:2). Our ability to prove faithful is a result of the Holy Spirit directing our efforts to act honorably, with integrity and trustworthiness, and to submit to our Lord's will, obediently and devotedly following His directives as we seek to serve others in His love. We can then say, along with the apostle Paul, "I thank Christ Jesus our Lord, who has given me strength, that he considered me trustworthy, appointing me to his service" (1 Timothy 1:12).

Gentleness – The prophet Isaiah describes the gentleness of our Lord Jesus using the analogy of a tender-hearted shepherd, stating, "He tends his flock like a shepherd: He gathers the lambs in his arms and carries them close to his heart; he gently leads those that have young" (Isaiah 40:11). Some 700 years later, Jesus said of Himself: "I am the good shepherd. The good shepherd lays down his life for the sheep" (John 10:11). Jesus, our good shepherd, displayed a heart for humanity that was so loving, gentle, kind, and tender – yet, unbreakably strong – that He sacrificed His life to save us. Calling upon each of us to follow the example He set for us, our Lord and Savior tells us, "Take my yoke upon you and learn from me, for I am gentle and humble in heart" (Matthew 11:29).

As we seek to follow our Lord's directive, it is important to remember that underlying our Savior's gentle and humble heart were both deep love and tremendous strength – strength of character, righteousness, and the unwavering conviction to stand lovingly, firmly and faithfully in obedience to God. Therefore, with divine help from the Holy Spirit, we, too, will become strong enough to be gentle – possessing a tender, loving heart for others, a faithful commitment to our Lord and Savior, and the ever-increasing ability to "let [our] gentleness be evident to all" (Philippians 4:5, emphasis mine).

Self-Control – Our Lord and Savior faced many situations throughout His life on earth that must have profoundly offended and, at times, deeply angered Him. One of the most difficult of these occasions surely must have been standing before a murderous crowd, duplicitous high priests, and a corrupt governor who falsely accused, mocked, and abused Him. Even so, with extraordinary self-control, Jesus stood quietly, calmly, and respectfully before them all. He conducted Himself with the utmost grace, integrity, honor, and humility during the most vicious and violent circumstances imaginable. In doing so, He set for us the perfect example of self-control – an example He wants very much for each one of us to follow.

Our self-control is challenged all day, every day, in a myriad of ways. We are bombarded by media that entices, seduces, and challenges us to engage in worldly behaviors openly. Tempers and tongues run wild. Angry outbursts are commonplace. Vulgarity seems to have become part of normal speech. Nudity and sexuality are flaunted without restraint. In this "me-first" culture of today, people don't see the need to hold back. Nevertheless, as followers of Christ, we must live differently if we desire to make a difference on His behalf. We must hold fast to what our Lord has taught us and constantly "Be alert and of sober mind" because, as the apostle Peter goes on to point out, "your enemy the devil prowls around like a roaring lion looking for someone to devour" (1 Peter 5:8).

Satan is relentless with his tantalizing bombardment of temptations. Outside influences, as well as internal desires, are a constant battle for each of us. However, because we are followers of Christ indwelt and empowered by the Holy Spirit, we can stand firm, practice self-control, and do what is right in God's eyes. The apostle Paul reminds us, "Those who belong to Christ Jesus have crucified the flesh with its passions and desires. Since we live by the Spirit, let us keep in step with the Spirit" (Galatians 5:24-25).

The Holy Spirit lives within the hearts and minds of all believers. He is our constant advocate, helper, guide, encourager, counselor, and teacher. He enables us to faithfully follow our Lord Jesus' instructions and carry out His commands with love, joy, peace, patience, kindness, goodness, faithfulness, gentleness, and self-control. Therefore, as the apostle Paul wisely counsels, "Do not stifle the Holy Spirit" (1 Thessalonians 5:19 NLT).

In addition to the Holy Spirit endowing us with the spiritual fruit listed above, He also equips every believer with one or more unique spiritual gifts. In a letter to the early Corinthian believers, the apostle Paul explains, "There are different kinds of spiritual gifts, but the same Spirit is the source of them all. There are different kinds of service, but we serve the same Lord. God works in different ways, but it is the same God who does the work in all of us. A spiritual gift is given to each of us, so we can help each other. To one person the Spirit gives the ability to give wise advice; to another the same Spirit gives a message of special knowledge. The same Spirit gives great faith to another, and to someone else the one Spirit gives the gift of healing. He gives one person the power to perform miracles, and another the ability to prophesy. He gives someone else the ability to discern whether a message is from the Spirit of God or from another spirit. Still another person is given the ability to speak in unknown languages, while another is given the ability to interpret what is being said. It is the one and only Spirit who distributes all these gifts. He alone decides which gift each person should have" (1 Corinthians 12:4-11 NLT). Therefore, as the apostle Peter tells us, "Each of you should use whatever gift you have received to serve others, as faithful stewards of God's grace in its various forms" (1 Peter 4:10).

PRAYER

Prayer is our most crucial lifeline to God, and it is the most direct line of communication we have with our Creator and Savior. As such, the apostle Paul reminds us that we should "pray without ceasing, in everything give thanks; for this is the will of God in Christ Jesus for you" (1 Thessalonians 5:17-18 NKJV).

Through prayer, we receive our Lord's strength, direction, guidance, and wisdom. It is how we cry out to God for help, support, comfort, healing, and forgiveness. "Is anyone among you in trouble? Let them pray," directs James, our Lord's brother; because, as he goes on to tell us, "The prayer of a righteous person is powerful and effective" (James 5:13, 16). Whatever we ask for through prayer in Jesus' name, (that is, in accordance with the will of God), we know we will receive it. "If you ask anything in my name," our Lord Jesus assures us, "I will do it" (John 14:14 NKJV).

Prayer draws us close to God, allows us to hear His voice, ask for His help, seek His blessings, thank Him, and praise Him – just as Jesus did throughout His life on earth. It is also the most powerful way for us to ask God to work in the lives of others. As such, the apostle Paul gives us this advice: "Devote yourselves to prayer, being watchful and thankful ... Pray in the Spirit on all occasions with all kinds of prayers and requests. With this in mind, be alert and always keep on praying for all the Lord's people" (Colossians 4:2; Ephesians 6:18).

Although we may know how important prayer is, we may still experience times when we find it very difficult, if not seemingly impossible, to pray. Perhaps we don't know what, specifically, to pray for or how to ask God to meet our needs or to help someone else. There may also be times when we just don't have the emotional strength to pray. I, very painfully, experienced this one Christmas as I prayed over my youngest son. He had become critically ill, was on life-support, and not expected to survive. After earnestly praying over him every day for nearly two weeks, I awoke one morning and found I could not pray. I was exhausted, overwhelmed, and depleted; and, at that moment I could neither organize my thoughts nor find any words for prayer. That day, God graciously sent others to my side who not only prayed for my son but prayed for me as well. Our Lord renewed my strength, and, in time, blessedly, healed my son.

Fortunately, in every situation, the Holy Spirit is there to help us and knows precisely what is needed, even when we, or others, can't ask God for it. As the apostle Paul explains, "The Holy Spirit helps us in our weakness. For example, we don't know what God wants us to pray for. But the Holy Spirit prays for us with groanings that cannot be expressed in words. And the Father who knows all hearts knows what the Spirit is saying, for the Spirit pleads for us believers in harmony with God's own will" (Romans 8:26-27 NLT). Ever faithful, compassionate, and caring, our loving Creator graciously provides a way to cover all our communication bases with Him!

FELLOW BELIEVERS (THE BODY OF CHRIST)

We, along with all our brothers and sisters in Christ, are members of

His worldwide church. The apostle Paul tells us, "All of you together are Christ's body, and each of you is a part of it" (1 Corinthians 12:27 NLT). Although we differ in many ways and receive varying degrees of faith, gifts, abilities, wisdom, and understanding, together we comprise the unified body of our Lord and Savior here on earth. And just as the human body is made up of many parts, each one important to and dependent upon the others, we, as the body of Christ, also need and are dependent upon one another. The apostle Paul, therefore, teaches us to pray: "May the God who gives endurance and encouragement give [us] the same attitude of mind toward each other that Christ Jesus had, so that with one mind and one voice [we] may glorify the God and Father of our Lord Jesus Christ" (Romans 15:5-6, emphasis mine).

Christian fellowship not only allows us to share our faith and refresh our spirits by worshipping God together, but it can also be an excellent source of encouragement, comfort, healing, and hope when we face the many trials and difficulties of life in this sinful, fallen world. "Let us consider how we may spur one another on toward love and good deeds," writes the author of Hebrews, "not giving up meeting together, as some are in the habit of doing, but encouraging one another – and all the more as you see the Day approaching" (Hebrews 10:24-25).

Today we see enormous divisions in our churches, an overwhelming number of false teachers and false teachings, and blatant, rampant rebellion against God and His Word. As such, it is imperative for us, as the faithful followers of Christ Jesus, to build each other up and strengthen one another in the Truth to help protect each other from falling into sin, being misled, making wrong choices, or compromising our faith. "Therefore encourage one another and build each other up, just as in fact you are doing" advises the apostle Paul. "Let the message of Christ dwell among you richly as you teach and admonish one another with all wisdom through psalms, hymns, and songs from the Spirit, singing to God with gratitude in your hearts. And whatever you do, whether in word or deed, do it all in the name of the Lord Jesus, giving thanks to God the Father through him" (1 Thessalonians 5:11; Colossians 3:16-17).

As we have seen throughout this chapter, our Lord graciously and divinely provides all the resources necessary to equip each one of us to love Him and love our neighbors just as He has commanded us to do. The question, then, is not whether we will be *able* to live in God's love, but whether we are *willing* to live in His love.

A Word

"But the wisdom that comes from heaven is first of all pure; then peace-loving, considerate, submissive, full of mercy and good fruit, impartial and sincere" (James 3:17).

And A Prayer

"May the grace of the Lord Jesus Christ, and the love of God, and the fellowship of the Holy Spirit be with you all" (2 Corinthians 13:14).

CHAPTER FIVE
THE ATTITUDES AND ATTRIBUTES OF LIVING IN LOVE

WHILE GOD HAS GRACIOUSLY and lovingly provided all the resources we need to faithfully and joyfully live in His love, whether we opt to use the tools He has given to us is a choice that each of us must make, sometimes multiple times within a single day, as we face the ever-changing situations and circumstances in our lives. Our decisions, individually and collectively, not only influence the direction our lives will take on any given day, they ultimately determine our future, the relationship we have with our Lord and Savior, how effective we will be as His ambassadors, and the kind of relationships we have with others.

Because each of our choices has such a significant impact on our lives, as well as the lives of others, it is essential for us to understand how we come to make the choices we do. Every choice we make begins with a single thought. Each individual thought (idea, image, impression, etc.) then works together with other thoughts to form our attitudes. Our attitudes determine and direct the decisions we make. Our decisions, in turn, result in the words we speak and the actions we take. As such, everything we say and do is merely the outward expression of the attitudes we hold as determined by our innermost thoughts. King Solomon wisely states, "For as [a person] thinks in his heart, so is he" (Proverbs 23:7 NKJV, emphasis mine). Or, in modern terms: we are what we think.

We are what we think follows the same basic principle found in the expression *you are what you eat*. Whatever we put into our bodies has a significant impact on our health. If we consume a steady diet of junk food, soda, sweets, fats, and carbohydrates we can expect to become overweight and develop significant health problems like diabetes, high cholesterol, and heart disease. If, on the other hand, we consume a moderate diet rich in healthy foods like fresh lean meats, fish, fruits, and vegetables we can expect to have healthier bodies, more energy, and live longer, more productive lives. In the same way, what we feed our minds profoundly impacts the attitudes we develop and the subsequent actions we take. For example, if we put evil, sinful thoughts into our minds, indulge in negative thinking or ruminate on unpleasant memories, etc. we are likely to become mentally and emotionally unhealthy people. We are also much more likely to be depressed, discouraged, and destructive people with unpleasant dispositions.

As a former human resource professional, I can attest to how detrimental bad attitudes can be. Not only do they adversely impact the person who has the unhealthy mindset, but they can also, and often do, negatively affect those around them causing conflict, discord, and loss of productivity. As my grandmother used to say, "One bad apple can spoil the whole barrel." As Christians, the followers of Christ Jesus and His chosen ambassadors, we must be especially careful not to get drawn into harmful, unhealthy, or hateful attitudes and make sure we are not the bad apples in the barrel.

The best way for us to combat negative and destructive thoughts and stem bad attitudes is to fill our minds with thoughts that are wholesome, positive, and godly. "Brothers and sisters, whatever is true, whatever is noble, whatever is right, whatever is pure, whatever is lovely, whatever is admirable – if anything is excellent or praiseworthy – think about such things," counsels the apostle Paul (Philippians 4:8).

OUR THOUGHTS SET THE COURSE FOR OUR LIVES

If we are what we think, and we think about virtuous and godly things, we will not only become the kind of people our Lord intends for us to be, we will enjoy good mental, emotional, and spiritual health. Likewise, if we fill our minds with inappropriate, evil, or immoral thoughts that do not reflect God's Word and Jesus' teaching our mental, emotional, and spiritual health will decline and our witness for Christ Jesus will be severely compromised, if not destroyed altogether. Our Lord and Savior tells us plainly, "A good [person] brings good things out of the good stored up in him, and the evil [person] brings evil things out of the evil stored up in him" (Matthew 12:35, emphasis mine).

"Those who live according to the flesh have their minds set on what that nature desires," writes the apostle Paul, "but those who live in accordance with the Spirit have their minds set on what the Spirit desires" (Romans 8:5). Since what we produce in our lives is solely the result of the thought-choices we make all day long, every day, "Don't copy the behavior and customs of this world, but let God transform you into a new person by changing the way you think," instructs Paul. "Then you will learn to know God's will for you, which is good and pleasing and perfect" (Romans 12:2 NLT).

ADOPTING NEW CHRISTLIKE THOUGHTS AND ATTITUDES

God's good, pleasing, and perfect will is that we continue to focus our hearts and minds on loving and serving Him and not on this sinful world and all its trappings. "Since, then, you have been raised with Christ," states Paul, "set your hearts on things above, where Christ is, seated at the right hand of God. Set your minds on things above, not on earthly things" (Colossians 3:1-2).

As Jesus' followers and the redeemed, heaven-bound children of almighty God, we must think and act differently than those whose minds and hearts are still engaged in sinful actions and unhealthy earthly pursuits. "You were taught, with regard to your former way of life," admonishes the apostle Paul, "to put off your old self, which is being corrupted by its deceitful desires; to be made new in the attitude of your minds; and to put on the new self, created to be like God in true righteousness and holiness" (Ephesians 4:22-24).

Our new self and our new attitudes are the result of the new life we are born into when we accept Jesus as our Lord and Savior. "I tell you the truth," Jesus told Nicodemus, "unless you are born again, you cannot see the Kingdom of God" (John 3:3 NLT). Being "born again" means that we are transformed into new people through our relationship with Christ Jesus and that we are indwelt by the very presence of God through His Holy Spirit. "God has given us his Spirit as proof that we live in him and he in us," affirms the apostle John (1 John 4:13 NLT). "This means that anyone who belongs to Christ has become a new person," explains the apostle Paul. "The old life is gone; a new life has begun!" (2 Corinthians 5:17 NLT)

LIVING OUR NEW LIVES

No matter how far down we may have fallen or what sins we may have committed in the past, we have a whole new life and identity when we accept Christ Jesus as Lord and Savior. As born-again believers, we are sanctified, or made holy, by Jesus' sacrifice and become saints, or "ones set apart," for Him. (Jesus' faithful followers are referred to as "saints" more than 50 times in the New Testament.) Our way of thinking, as well as our nature, conduct, and character, are forever changed through this new relationship we have with our Savior.

"Therefore," instructs the apostle Peter, "with minds that are alert and fully sober, set your hope on the grace to be brought to you when Jesus Christ is revealed at his coming. As obedient children, do not conform to the evil desires you had when you lived in ignorance. But just as he who called you is holy, so be holy in all you do; for it is written: 'Be holy, because I am holy'" (1 Peter 1:13-16).

Peter leaves no room for doubt as to what this means to us when he goes on to say, "You have had enough in the past of the evil things that godless people enjoy – their immorality and lust, their feasting and drunkenness and wild parties, and their terrible worship of idols. Of course, your former friends are surprised when you no longer plunge into the flood of wild and destructive things they do. So they slander you. But remember that they will have to face God, who stands ready to judge everyone, both the living and the dead" (1 Peter 4:3-5 NLT).

The apostle Paul has the same concerns in mind when he shares these words of wisdom and instruction, and a solemn warning: "So I say, walk by the Spirit, and you will not gratify the desires of the flesh. For the flesh desires what is contrary to the Spirit, and the Spirit what is contrary to the flesh. They are in conflict with each other, so that you are not to do whatever you want ... The acts of the flesh are obvious: sexual immorality, impurity and debauchery; idolatry and witchcraft; hatred, discord, jealousy, fits of rage, selfish ambition, dissensions, factions and envy; drunkenness, orgies, and the like. I warn you, as I did before, that those who live like this will not inherit the Kingdom of God ... Don't be fooled by those who try to excuse these sins, for the anger of God will fall on those who disobey Him ... For God did not call us to be impure, but to live a holy life. Therefore, anyone who rejects this instruction does not reject a human being but God, the very God who gives you his Holy Spirit" (Galatians 5:16-17, 19-21; Ephesians 5:6 NLT; 1 Thessalonians 4:7-8).

We have all, at times, had impure or improper thoughts and engaged in behaviors that were far below the new standards to which God has called us. We are relentlessly assailed with provocative, if not blatantly sexual images, graphic violence, foul language, and immorality in countless forms. We are often forced to see, hear, and experience the worst of human behavior and speech throughout our normal daily lives. It is nearly impossible today to filter out all the filth. Nevertheless, as followers of Christ Jesus, we must continually try to do just that.

"Don't you realize that those who do wrong will not inherit the Kingdom of God?" asks the apostle Paul. "Don't fool yourselves. Those who indulge in sexual sin, or who worship idols, or commit adultery, or are male prostitutes, or practice homosexuality, or are thieves, or greedy people, or drunkards, or are abusive, or cheat people – none of these will inherit the Kingdom of God. Some of you were once like that. But you were cleansed; you were made holy; you were made right with God by calling on the name of the Lord Jesus Christ and by the Spirit of our God" (1 Corinthians 6:9-11 NLT).

"So put to death the sinful, earthly things lurking within you" instructs Paul. "Have nothing to do with sexual immorality, impurity, lust, and evil desires. Don't be greedy, for a greedy person is an idolater, worshiping the things of this world. Because of these sins, the anger of God is coming. You used to do these things when your life was still part of this world. But now is the time to get rid of anger, rage, malicious behavior, slander, and dirty language. Don't lie to each other, for you have stripped off your old sinful nature and all its wicked deeds. Put on your new nature, and be renewed as you learn to know your Creator and become like him" (Colossians 3:5-10 NLT).

Just as it wouldn't make sense for us to take off the dirty, sweaty clothes we wore to work in the yard on a sweltering summer day and then put them back on again after taking a cool, cleansing shower; it also doesn't make sense for us, as the followers of Christ Jesus, to continue to engage in corrupt thinking or immoral behavior after being purified through the sacrifice He made to give us a brand new life. As such, we must shed our old lives, along with any sinful thoughts, attitudes, and actions, and put on our new, Christlike lives, adopting His thoughts, attitudes, and actions as our own.

This new lifestyle applies to all Christians, no matter who we are, where we come from, what church we attend, how well educated we may or may not be, or how much money we may or may not have. The apostle Paul reminds us, "In this new life, it doesn't matter if you are a Jew or a Gentile [race or religion], circumcised or uncircumcised [religious affiliation], barbaric, uncivilized [education or culture], slave, or free [social class, poverty or wealth]. Christ is all that matters, and he lives in all of us." (Colossians 3:11 NLT, emphasis mine).

THINKING THE WAY JESUS THINKS LEADS TO LIVING CHRISTLIKE LIVES

Our Creator's image has been impressed upon the hearts and minds of all believers by the Holy Spirit through our relationship with Christ Jesus; and as a result, the apostle Paul tells us "we have the mind of Christ" (1 Corinthians 2:16 NKJV). Because we have the mind of our Lord at work within us, Paul assures us, "We [are able to] demolish arguments and every pretension that sets itself up against the knowledge of God, and we [can] take captive every thought to make it obedient to Christ" (2 Corinthians 10:5, emphasis mine).

Taking control over our thoughts so that we can live Christlike lives requires that we continually input godly information by reading and meditating upon God's Word and prayerfully asking Him to help us apply it to our lives. Taking God's Word into our hearts and minds each day is the mental and spiritual equivalent of putting nourishing food into our bodies each day. Without spiritual food, we cannot grow in the wisdom and knowledge of God, develop Christlike attitudes, or cultivate Christlike character. Depriving our minds of God's Word and Jesus' teaching will cause us to spiritually wither and die, just as denying our bodies food would eventually cause us to die of starvation.

Thinking Christlike thoughts is, therefore, an essential prerequisite to living Christlike lives. If we want to emulate our Lord, the apostle Paul tells us, "You must have the same attitude that Christ Jesus had" (Philippians 2:5 NLT). Jesus' attitude was unfailingly one of loving self-sacrifice, humble obedience, and the desire to faithfully serve His heavenly Father in every way – even to the point of sacrificing His life to save sinful humankind. Consequently, for our attitude to be the same as that of Christ Jesus, we must strip off our old lives and follow His example, putting on, or incorporating into our own lives, the attributes, or virtues, which are representative of a loving, faithful, humble, obedient, and self-sacrificing servant.

"Therefore, as God's chosen people, holy and dearly loved, clothe yourselves with compassion, kindness, humility, gentleness and patience" directs the apostle Paul. "Bear with each other and forgive one another if any of you has a grievance against someone. Forgive as the Lord forgave you. And over all these virtues put on love, which binds them all together in perfect unity" (Colossians 3:12-14). These seven virtues, which are all attributes of our Lord and Savior, in combination with the development of Christlike thoughts and attitudes, are what will enable us to put our Lord's love into action. Let's take a closer look at what it means to "clothe ourselves" with each of these virtues and how developing and implementing them will help us to become more loving and faithful ambassadors for Christ Jesus.

COMPASSION (TENDER HEARTED MERCY)

James, our Lord's brother, states, "The Lord is full of compassion and mercy" (James 5:11). Compassion is one of the most powerful and prominent components of both God's character and His love for us. It is because He loved us so deeply that God was moved with compassion to save us from the grip of sin and death.

God continues to show us what it means to be compassionate by providing comfort and care as we face the many trials and tragedies in our lives. As we experience the compassion and comfort of God, it stirs within us the same ability to be compassionate and provide comfort to others. The apostle Paul writes, "Praise be to the God and Father of our Lord Jesus Christ, the Father of compassion and the God of all comfort, who comforts us in all our troubles, so that we can comfort those in any trouble with the comfort we ourselves receive from God" (2 Corinthians 1:3-4).

Not only do we become more compassionate people through our personal experiences of receiving compassion from God, but we also have the extraordinary examples of Jesus' compassion to follow. Our Lord continually provided compassionate care and comfort to people who were suffering, broken-hearted, and in need. He demonstrated tenderness, heartfelt sympathy, and merciful kindness toward everyone with whom He had contact. Our Lord fed the hungry, healed the sick, and even brought the dead back to life.

Luke, the physician-evangelist, tells us about a particular instance when Jesus encountered a young widow who had just lost her only son: "When the Lord saw her, his heart overflowed with compassion. 'Don't cry!' he said. Then he walked over to the coffin and touched it, and the bearers stopped. 'Young man,' he said, 'I tell you, get up.' Then the dead boy sat up and began to talk! And Jesus gave him back to his mother" (Luke 7:13-15 NLT). Jesus felt great compassion for this grieving mother and was deeply moved to both comfort her and change her circumstances.

One of the things I find most compelling about Jesus' compassion is that it often included physical touch. Our Savior was affectionate. Without question, Jesus touched people's hearts and minds with His words and actions, but He also touched people physically to convey the depth of His love and compassionate concern for them. Our Lord didn't need to touch people to comfort or heal them; rather, He chose to touch them because He wanted to have a deeper, more personal connection with them. This was true even with those no one else would ever touch.

The apostle Mark recalls, "A man with leprosy [a highly contagious and deadly disease] came and knelt in front of Jesus, begging to be healed. 'If you are willing, you can heal me and make me clean,' he said. Moved with compassion, Jesus reached out and touched him. 'I am willing,' he said. 'Be healed'" (Mark 1:40-41 NLT, emphasis mine). Our Savior didn't hesitate to touch the sick, diseased, disabled, or even the dead, offering them both His loving compassion and kind-hearted affection.

Our Lord, leading by example, let us know that hurting people benefit from compassionate human touch. A gentle hug, the touch of a hand, an arm around a shoulder, or a pat on the back are all expressions of support, encouragement, and comfort that lovingly convey genuine care and concern when they are *appropriately* and *respectfully* given.

As we can see, clothing ourselves with the virtue of compassion goes far beyond feeling sympathy or empathy for someone. Compassion doesn't just tug on our heartstrings; it moves us to take action and do whatever we can, to the greatest extent possible, to meet the physical, emotional, and spiritual needs of those who are suffering.

KINDNESS

As we already know from the preceding chapters, kindness is both an attribute of God and evidence that the Holy Spirit is working within us. The kindnesses we demonstrate to others are, therefore, a reflection of God's love and presence in our lives, and representative of the love He has for all people.

Demonstrating kindness, like compassion, means that we graciously and generously care for others and meet their needs with sincere warmth, gentleness, thoughtfulness, understanding, forbearance, and consideration whenever we have an opportunity to do so.

The ways for us to clothe ourselves with the virtue of kindness are virtually unlimited. They may be as small as bestowing a smile on someone to brighten their day or as immense as meeting a critical life need. Every genuine expression of kindness, however great or small, is both an act of Christlike love and an expression of God's grace.

HUMILITY

As we learned in Chapter Three, humility does not come easy for us. Nevertheless, the apostle Peter tells us, "All of you, clothe yourselves with humility toward one another, because, 'God opposes the proud but shows favor to the humble'" (1 Peter 5:5).

It is helpful for us to remember that true humility begins by living in submission to God out of reverent love for Him, and with the full knowledge that it is by His will alone we live and breathe; and that it is by His love and grace alone that we are saved. This understanding of our position, and the position of all humankind, should not only foster deep humility within us, but as Christians, we should also be extremely thankful because we know that submitting to our Lord's will in everything will ultimately lift us up to the very heights of heaven. Peter goes on to tell us, "Humble yourselves, therefore, under God's mighty hand, that he may lift you up in due time" (1 Peter 5:6).

Only when we sincerely humble ourselves before God and open our hearts to Him can He develop true humility within us. King David reminds us, "[God] guides the humble in what is right and teaches them his way" (Psalm 25:9, emphasis mine). God's way, of course, was evidenced throughout the life of Christ Jesus who demonstrated every aspect of true humility.

As Jesus illustrated for us, clothing ourselves with the virtue of humility means setting aside our pride, our concerns for recognition, personal advancement, and self-centered goals in favor of the caring and protective love that selflessly seeks the best for others. It means building others up, encouraging their hearts in love, and putting their needs ahead of our own. To humbly take a lesser place to advance the needs and welfare of another person is an act of genuine Christlike love.

GENTLENESS

The apostle Paul tells us to "be completely humble and gentle" (Ephesians 4:2). As we learned in Chapter Four, Jesus describes Himself as gentle and humble in heart, two attributes that go hand-in-hand, and instructs us to learn to practice these virtues from the example He set for us.

As we follow our Lord's directive and look at how He lived, we see that His humility led Him to be exceedingly gentle, even in the most difficult and painful circumstances. In turn, His gentle nature was the outward evidence of His humility. Our Savior shows us that we cannot effectively have one of these virtues without the other. Therefore, it stands to reason that we cannot be pompous, self-righteous, arrogant, and overbearing while at the same time being gentle, soft-spoken, tender-hearted, and kind.

Without gentleness, it would be quite difficult, if not impossible, for us to be credible witnesses for our Lord and Savior. As such, the apostle Peter advises, "In your hearts revere Christ as Lord. Always be prepared to give an answer to everyone who asks you to give the reason for the hope that you have. But do this with gentleness and respect" (1 Peter 3:15).

The apostle Paul reminds us, "A servant of the Lord must not quarrel but must be kind to everyone, be able to teach, and be patient with difficult people. Gently instruct those who oppose the truth. Perhaps God will change those people's hearts, and they will learn the truth." (2 Timothy 2:24-25 NLT).

Gentleness can open doors that allow us to share God's love and the gospel message with people who might otherwise be resistant to them, especially when our gentleness comes from a loving heart that desires to encourage and care for others rather than convict or control them.

Gentleness softens hardened hearts, makes friends out of enemies, pursues peaceful negotiations, and diffuses tempers when we face others' anger, hostility, and hatefulness.

The virtue of gentleness, guided by God's love, embodies tenderness, thoughtfulness, consideration, and sensitivity toward the feelings and needs of others; it demonstrates kindness and practices patience under even the most trying of circumstances. It is, therefore, one of the most powerful attributes of Christlike love and why the apostle Paul writes, "Pursue righteousness and a godly life, along with faith, love, perseverance, and gentleness" (1 Timothy 6:11 NLT).

PATIENCE (LONG-SUFFERING)

As we have come to understand in Chapters Three and Four, patience is both a principal attribute of God's love for us and a gracious working of the Holy Spirit within us. Our Lord has extraordinary patience with us, waiting with loving-kindness for us to come to Him, learn from Him, be obedient to Him, and become the people He desires for us to be. God sees the ruin and chaos, the harm we do to ourselves, others, and the world; and still, He is patient with us.

The apostle Paul, using himself as an example, describes what our Lord's patience means to all of us. He writes, "Here is a trustworthy saying that deserves full acceptance: Christ Jesus came into the world to save sinners – of whom I am the worst. But for that very reason I was shown mercy so that in me, the worst of sinners, Christ Jesus might display his immense patience as an example for those who would believe in him and receive eternal life" (1 Timothy 1:15-16). As patient as our Lord is with us, how can we possibly refuse to be patient with one another?

The apostle Paul urges us to "be patient with everyone" (1 Thessalonians 5:14). However, as we know, the virtue of patience is one of the most difficult to develop and put into practice, especially in this fast-paced, high-stress world we live in today.

Being patient means that we remain composed and self-controlled, with dignity and grace, in the face of other's hurtful or frustrating behavior, anger, or ill-treatment. It means that we stay calm through the many trials, disappointments, challenges, and suffering that occur in our day-to-day lives. Patience is what allows us to find serenity in times of stress and enables us to persevere under life's daily provocations and pressures.

The familiar adage "patience is a virtue" dates to a poem believed to have been written back in the 5th century. Even so, these words remain as valid and vital today as they did thousands of years ago. When we clothe ourselves with the virtue of patience, in addition to humility, compassion, kindness, and gentleness, we will have more peace within ourselves and more peaceful interactions with others, even with those people who might otherwise thrive on promoting conflict.

BEAR WITH EACH OTHER (FORBEARANCE)

The apostle Paul tells us, "Carry each other's burdens, and in this way you will fulfill the law of Christ" (Galatians 6:2). The law of Christ, as we know, is the law of love. When we bear with others, making allowances for their faults, failures, and shortcomings, we are demonstrating the sacrificial love our Lord requires of us and that He exhibits toward each one of us.

We all have weaknesses, bad habits, and irritating or undesirable behaviors and need others to bear with us at times. Keeping in mind our own less than desirable qualities, we should maintain a humble attitude that reminds us to be more patient, kind, and compassionate, and less grudging and judgmental, when we experience others' flaws and failures.

When we clothe ourselves with the virtue of forbearance we kindly, gently, and lovingly bear with people when they are not at their best and, at times, when they are at their worst. As Jesus so graciously bears with us, we, too, must patiently endure the blunders, suffer through slights and selfishness, pardon mistakes, and put up with others' affronts and offenses with grace, dignity, and respect; and always "[bear] with one another in love" (Ephesians 4:2, emphasis mine).

FORGIVE (AS WE ARE FORGIVEN)

The apostle Paul writes, "Be kind to each other, tenderhearted, forgiving one another, just as God through Christ has forgiven you" (Ephesians 4:32 NLT). In His mercy and love, God sacrificed His own Son, Christ Jesus, who had never committed a single sin, so that we could be forgiven of the countless sins we commit throughout our lives. Unlike our sinless Lord and Savior, the author of Ecclesiastes reminds all of us, "There is no one on earth who is righteous, no one who does what is right and never sins" (Ecclesiastes 7:20). We are all sinners saved by God's grace.

Given the extraordinary degree to which God has forgiven each of us, we should not only understand our Lord's requirement that we forgive one another, we should sincerely *want* to forgive one another. Unfortunately, we know that isn't always the case, especially when someone keeps repeating the same sin(s) over and over again. We get frustrated, discouraged, and, sometimes, angered by such behavior. Nevertheless, Jesus has a rule we must follow. He tells us, "Even if they sin against you seven times in a day and seven times come back to you saying 'I repent,' you must forgive them" (Luke 17:4). As difficult as this may be for us to do, we are required to forgive others without limit. As we learned in Chapter Three, "love…keeps no record of being wronged" (1 Corinthians 13:5 NLT).

If we want God to forgive us for our sins, we must be willing to forgive those who sin against us. Our Lord explains in the book of Matthew, "If you forgive other people when they sin against you, your heavenly Father will also forgive you. But if you do not forgive others their sins, your Father will not forgive your sins" (Matthew 6:14-15).

God willingly, immediately, and completely forgives us when we sincerely confess our sins and ask for His forgiveness with a genuinely repentant heart. However, if we refuse to forgive someone else for a wrong they have committed against us, we are disobeying God and as such, actively engaging in sin. As a result, we remain in an unforgiven state. For this reason, Jesus tells us, "When you stand praying, if you hold anything against anyone, forgive them, so that your Father in heaven may forgive you your sins" (Mark 11:25).

Refusing to forgive someone not only separates us from God through sin, but it also damages our walk and relationship with our Lord and Savior, keeps us in bondage to Satan, robs us of peace, ruins our relationships with others, and renders our witness as ambassadors for Christ Jesus null and void. Unforgiveness is also an act of pride and rebellion against God. It leads to bitterness, anger, resentment, unkindness, impatience, hard-heartedness, sorrow, and suffering – our own as well as others.

The choice to forgive, on the other hand, draws us closer to God, frees us from bondage to sin, and gives us peace with God, peace within ourselves, and peace with others. Forgiveness doesn't mean we condone evil or hurtful acts, that we no longer care about such things or turn a blind eye to them. Instead, it means that we trust God to justly and rightly deal with the person and their sin. He will not let sin go unpunished. The apostle Paul warns, "Do not repay anyone evil for evil … Do not take revenge, my dear friends, but leave room for God's wrath, for it is written: 'It is mine to avenge; I will repay,' says the Lord" (Romans 12:17, 19).

Genuine Christlike forgiveness is also no-strings-attached forgiveness. It doesn't make demands or set conditions before being given. Jesus never said, "I'll forgive you if you never mess up again, can be perfect from now on, will never make another mistake, or commit another sin." Rather, the apostle John tells us how easy Jesus makes it for us to receive His forgiveness. John states, "If we confess our sins, He is faithful and just to forgive us our sins and to cleanse us from all unrighteousness" (1 John 1:9 NKJV).

Additionally, true forgiveness means that we don't harbor ill-will or hold grudges. When God forgives us, He wipes our slate completely clean. To everyone He forgives, our heavenly Father makes the following irrefutable promise: "[Your] sins and lawless acts I will remember no more" (Hebrews 10:17, emphasis mine). Our Lord expects us to do the same.

Finally, forgiveness is the choice not to withhold our love. The apostle Peter tells us, "Above all, love each other deeply, because love covers over a multitude of sins" (1 Peter 4:8).

The combination of love and forgiveness can heal hearts and change lives in the most astounding ways. When I was in Rwanda in 2007, I came to understand, first-hand, how life-changing true forgiveness, covered by love, can be even in the most unimaginable circumstances. One afternoon, as we were listening to villager accounts of reconciliation, a local minister, Pastor Gahigi, and a man named Sendegeya told the story of how, during the 1994 genocide that took the lives of nearly a million people, Sendegeya had slaughtered six members of pastor Gahigi's family with a machete. Sendegeya was put in prison where, eventually, pastor Gahigi went to visit him. Pastor Gahigi told Sendegeya that God forgave him, and so did he. Through the course of many visits, the two men shared Scripture and talked about what had happened. Sendegeya sincerely apologized and repented for what he had done. Years later, when Sendegeya was released from prison, pastor Gahigi took him into his own home as a beloved friend and brother in Christ. It is where Sendegeya still lives today.

There were many other remarkable stories told during my visit, including that of an elderly woman who took the man who killed her entire family into her home, not only forgiving him, but also telling him that to make amends he would have to become her "son," her family, in place of those he had murdered. He agreed; and, in time, they forged a close, loving relationship. These stories are reminders to all of us that "with God nothing will be impossible" – not even forgiving the seemingly unforgivable (Luke 1:37 NKJV).

King David writes, "O Lord, you are so good, so ready to forgive, so full of unfailing love for all who ask for your help" (Psalm 86:5 NLT). Since God loves us this deeply and forgives all our sins so completely, how could we not clothe ourselves with the virtue of forgiveness and lovingly forgive others as He has done for us?

LOVE

The virtues of compassion, kindness, humility, gentleness, patience, forbearance, and forgiveness are intrinsically woven together and bound by love. They are individually and collectively, independently and interdependently the outward expression of the thoughts we have, the attitudes we develop, and the actions we take.

As we allow the Holy Spirit to transform our hearts and minds, continue to study God's Word, and follow the example set for us by Jesus, the attitudes and attributes of godly love will be increasingly evident in our lives and our character. We will be ever more ready and able to fulfill our Lord and Savior's commandment to love others as He loved us, fulfill our role as His ambassadors, and live faithfully in His love.

A Word

"Guard your heart above all else, for it determines the course of your life" (Proverbs 4:23 NLT).

And A Prayer

"I pray that out of his glorious riches he may strengthen you with power through his Spirit in your inner being, so that Christ may dwell in your hearts through faith" (Ephesians 3:16-17).

CHAPTER SIX

LOVE IN ACTION

THE APOSTLE JOHN WRITES, "This is how we know what love is: Jesus Christ laid down his life for us. And we ought to lay down our lives for our brothers and sisters. If anyone has material possessions and sees a brother or sister in need but has no pity on them, how can the love of God be in that person? Dear children, let us not love with words or speech but with actions and in truth" (1 John 3:16-18).

James, our Lord's brother, asks similar questions: "What good is it, dear brothers and sisters, if you say you have faith but don't show it by your actions? Can that kind of faith save anyone? Suppose you see a brother or sister who has no food or clothing, and you say, 'Good-bye and have a good day; stay warm and eat well' – but then you don't give that person any food or clothing. What good does that do? So you see, faith by itself isn't enough. Unless it produces good deeds, it is dead and useless ... Just as the body is dead without breath, so also faith is dead without good works" (James 2:14-17, 26 NLT).

The apostle Paul provides a comprehensive answer to the questions above in a single statement: "The only thing that counts is faith expressing itself through love" (Galatians 5:6). Without expressing our faith in, and love for, our Lord and Savior through our actions it simply doesn't ring true. As we learned in Chapter Two, if we don't "walk our talk" by putting our love into action we will have no positive or credible witness as Jesus true followers.

In the preceding chapters, we covered a great deal of ground concerning the true (agape) love our Lord has called us to have for all the people He places in our lives: both fellow believers and unbelievers. We have looked at what love is, where it comes from, how God guides and enables it to grow in our lives, and how our thoughts and attitudes affect it. Along the way, we have grown to understand how living in love impacts those around us and how it can bring about changes in both our lives and the lives of others. In this chapter let's look at some additional Scripture verses that will help us put true charitable love into practice as we go about the normal activities of our daily lives.

LOVE MUST BE SINCERE (ROMANS 12:9)

Sincere love must be authentic, open, honest, and heartfelt. There can be no pretense, deceit, or hypocrisy in genuine love. Acts that may appear to be loving can sometimes be done for purely selfish reasons or stem from ulterior motives. Pretending to care about people, saying nice things, and exhibiting concern and compassion for others may look credible on the outside, yet not be heartfelt or sincere. God, however, always sees the real motivation behind our actions; and as the apostle John states, "If our hearts condemn us, we know that God is greater than our hearts, and he knows everything" (1 John 3:20). Almighty God is never in doubt as to our true motives. Therefore, as the apostle Peter tells us, "Love each other deeply with all your heart" (1 Peter 1:22 NLT).

DO GOOD TO EVERYONE

"As we have opportunity," instructs the apostle Paul, "let us do good to all people, especially to those who belong to the family of believers"

(Galatians 6:10). Doing good to *all* people means every person we encounter, from friends and family to strangers on the street, and, of course, to our brothers and sisters in Christ Jesus.

Doing good is a broad term that includes anything and everything that would bring Christlike love into people's lives. It may be something as simple as a warm smile or a kind word; providing food, clothing, or shelter; sharing the gospel message; providing needed instruction or discipline; or taking the necessary action to meet a critical life need. The apostle Paul reminds us, "[Christians] must learn to devote themselves to doing what is good, in order to provide for urgent needs and not live unproductive lives" (Titus 3:14, emphasis mine).

SHARE WITH THE LORD'S PEOPLE WHO ARE IN NEED (ROMANS 12:13)

The apostle John states clearly, "Anyone who has two shirts should share with the one who has none, and anyone who has food should do the same" (Luke 3:11). If we see someone in need and yet do nothing to help them we are, in essence, denying God's love to that person as well as, denying our love for God. King Solomon put it like this: "Whoever oppresses the poor shows contempt for their Maker, but whoever is kind to the needy honors God" (Proverbs 14:31).

Today, sharing with people in need is made not only easy but also convenient. We can contribute to food shelves, place needed items in drop boxes, and contribute financially through our churches, vetted charities, and other trusted organizations by effortlessly tapping a few keys on our phones or computers. We can donate clothing, furniture, and household goods to thrift stores and churches, or call a charity to pick them up. And, as we have the opportunity, we can personally give what's needed directly to those who need it – along with a smile, a gentle hug, and some kind words (as well as the gospel message if the Holy Spirit has impressed it upon our hearts to do so).

While we may have a generous heart for helping others, we must still do so responsibly and within our means. God does not require that we give beyond what we can afford nor give up what we truly need for ourselves or our own families. The apostle Paul rightly reminds us, "Give in proportion to what you have. Whatever you give is acceptable if you give it eagerly. And give according to what you have, not what you don't have" (2 Corinthians 8:11-12 NLT).

Whenever we do decide to give, it should always be done with both an open heart and an open hand. I first heard the expression "giving with an open hand" from my dear friends, Karen Runyan, (who has now gone to be with the Lord), and our beloved friend, "Buckie" Bookart. If you aren't familiar with this expression, it means to give joyfully, generously, and graciously without ever expecting to receive something in return.

With this in mind, the apostle Paul assures us, "Whoever sows sparingly will also reap sparingly, and whoever sows generously will also reap generously. Each of you should give what you have decided in your heart to give, not reluctantly or under compulsion, for God loves a cheerful giver. And God is able to bless you abundantly, so that in all things at all times, having all that you need, you will abound in every good work" (2 Corinthians 9:6-8).

Paul's words not only encourage us to give generously and gladly, but they also remind us that one day God will reward our efforts. Paul also tells us that if our hearts are open and we want to do good and give to others, God, by His grace, will not only make sure that we have what we need but that we will have enough to share.

Graciously sharing with others, tithing, and giving whatever we can to help others are not, however, all that we need to do when it comes to giving. "Give everyone what you owe them: If you owe taxes, pay taxes; if revenue, then revenue; if respect, then respect; if honor, then honor," instructs the apostle Paul (Romans 13:7).

Regardless of when, where, or how we give to and share with others, at the very heart of it all should be our love and gratitude for all that God has given, and continues to provide, for us. "This service that you perform is not only supplying the needs of the Lord's people," writes Paul, "but is also overflowing in many expressions of thanks to God" (2 Corinthians 9:12). Therefore, as the author of Hebrews encourages, "Do not forget to do good and to share, for with such sacrifices God is well pleased" (Hebrews 13:16 NKJV).

PRACTICE HOSPITALITY (ROMANS 12:13)

While the apostle Paul tells us to "practice hospitality," his colleague, the apostle Peter adds the following caveat: "Offer hospitality to one another *without grumbling*" (1 Peter 4:9, emphasis mine). How many times have we sighed when someone unexpectedly came to visit at an inopportune time or grumbled when extra people suddenly showed up for dinner? Peter clearly seems to understand how difficult it can be for us, at times, to be gracious in our hospitality!

Warmly and graciously welcoming others into our homes is what most of us commonly think of as offering hospitality. However, there is much more to practicing hospitality than inviting people in, hosting an event, or entertaining. Genuine hospitality is about opening our hearts and lives and letting people in – even if those people might be strangers to us. Hospitality provides a forum in which to share joys and sorrows, meet needs, provide encouragement, offer guidance, and, when appropriate, grant safe shelter to someone in need.

Although offering hospitality in its various forms is essential for us as followers of Christ, we must, nevertheless, be cautious and conscientious concerning our safety when offering any form of hospitality to others. There are no absolute guarantees that extending hospitality, opening our homes, or our hearts, to strangers, fellow believers, or even friends and family members will always be safe. Human beings are complex creatures living in a broken and sometimes violent world. We can't know for sure what might be going on in someone's mind or heart. Therefore, we need to be wise and discerning, and prayerfully ask God for His guidance, wisdom, and protection as appropriate.

REJOICE WITH THOSE WHO REJOICE; MOURN WITH THOSE WHO MOURN (ROMANS 12:15)

Jesus, always our perfect example, rejoiced with His friends and family members at a wedding celebration, sharing in their joy and performing His first miracle there. (John 2:1-11). Sharing in other's joy draws us closer to them and reinforces that their happiness is important to us.

Our Savior also experienced pain, sorrow, and loss. In the shortest verse in Scripture, the apostle John tells us that "Jesus wept" with his close friends, Mary and Martha, over the death of their beloved brother, Lazarus, who was one of our Lord's dearest friends. (John 11:35). Jesus knew how important it is to mourn with those whose hearts are broken and filled with sorrow.

With extraordinary loving-kindness, Jesus spoke to the grieving with compassion, reached out with tenderness to touch those who were suffering, and offered His comforting presence to the broken-hearted. King David reassures us, "The Lord is close to the brokenhearted; he rescues those whose spirits are crushed" (Psalm 34:18 NLT). Jesus did everything He could do to help others in their time of need; and we should strive to follow His example.

Whether we are sharing other's joys or sorrows, we know two fundamental things: first, God is always right here with us, and second, we can rejoice together in the knowledge that one day when we meet our Lord face-to-face, all our tears will be turned to joy! "[God] will wipe every tear from [our] eyes, and there will be no more death or sorrow or crying or pain," writes the apostle John. "All these things are gone forever" (Revelation 21:4 NLT, emphasis mine).

LIVE IN HARMONY WITH ONE ANOTHER (ROMANS 12:16)

The word harmony always reminds me of the exquisite music produced by a symphony orchestra or magnificent voices joining together in song. I once lived next door to a member of the famous a cappella group, the Blenders. They sometimes practiced very late at night, and while their music woke me up in the wee hours, I must admit the harmonies they created were wonderful as they melded their voices together, each member of the group complementing and working in concert with the others to create beautiful sounds.

This complementary collaboration reminds me that without mutual respect, appreciation of unique differences, and the desire to cooperate harmony cannot exist: in music or relationships. Imagine an orchestra in which the musicians who play the tuba and the trombone decide they are superior to the rest of the orchestra and put their own spin on the composition, completely disregarding the sheet music everyone else is following. Not only would it entirely ruin the music, but the entire orchestra would also be disgraced!

In the same way, respectfully working together, coordinating, accommodating, and humbly adapting to one another's needs enables us to live in harmony with each other. It gives us the ability to enjoy being with one another, to grow together, support one another, and accomplish the good things we are called to do as the body of Christ on earth. King David, knowing how important it is for us to live in harmony with each other, exclaims, "How good and pleasant it is when God's people live together in unity!" (Psalm 133:1).

However, the opposite is also true if we, as the followers of Christ Jesus, are not living in harmony with one another. When we treat each other unkindly and unlovingly, how could anyone possibly see the love of Jesus in us? If we fight and bicker, disagree with one another, are disrespectful, and say hateful things about each other, why would anyone want to be one of us?

Causing division among the followers of Christ is something Satan enjoys because it thoroughly destroys our witness, turns people off to God, and breeds sin in our lives. Understanding the real harm disunity causes, the apostle Peter counsels, "All of you should be of one mind. Sympathize with each other. Love each other as brothers and sisters. Be tenderhearted, and keep a humble attitude" (1 Peter 3:8 NLT).

Unfortunately, as we all know, there are endless divisions among professing Christians today. Some are relatively minor doctrinal differences, while others are blatant refusals to be obedient to our Lord's commands and severe breaches of Scripture. Therefore, while we must try to live harmoniously with our brothers and sisters in Christ, we must never compromise the truth of God's Word. And when necessary, we must heed the apostle Paul's advice, "Preach the word of God. Be prepared, whether the time is favorable or not. Patiently correct, rebuke, and encourage [God's] people with good teaching" (2 Timothy 4:2 NLT, emphasis mine).

Correcting another believer, (or anyone, for that matter), should always be done in the light of Jesus' love: firmly, yet, kindly, gently, patiently, and compassionately. A disposition of love strives to teach and nurture growth and understanding, and invites people to live rightly; while condemning or shaming others and demanding they change their ways usually produce only rebellion and rejection.

BE CAREFUL TO DO WHAT IS RIGHT IN THE EYES OF EVERYONE (ROMANS 12:17)

Moses states, "Do what is right and good in the Lord's sight, so all will go well with you" (Deuteronomy 6:18 NLT). The first step in doing what is right in the eyes of others is making sure we're first doing what is right in the eyes of God. Not only is God's standard of doing right our gold standard, but it is also, as we know, the standard by which we are identified as the true followers of Christ Jesus. The apostle John explains, "Dear children, don't let anyone deceive you about this: When people do what is right, it shows that they are righteous, even as Christ is righteous ... Anyone who does not live righteously and does not love other believers does not belong to God" (1 John 3:7, 10 NLT).

How do we define what it means to "do right"? James, our Lord's brother, gives us the answer: "If you really keep the royal law found in Scripture, 'Love your neighbor as yourself,' you are doing right" (James 2:8). Therefore, as the apostle Paul tells us, "brothers and sisters, never get tired of doing good" (2 Thessalonians 3:13).

BE AN EXAMPLE TO ALL BELIEVERS IN WHAT YOU SAY, IN THE WAY YOU LIVE, IN YOUR LOVE, YOUR FAITH, AND YOUR PURITY (1 TIMOTHY 4:12 NLT)

You and I, along with all our brothers and sisters in Christ, struggle daily against sin, evil influences, false teachings, worldliness, and the problems, stresses, and heartaches that come with living in this broken and sinful world. The temptations we face are around every corner, on every computer, and in an endless stream of media. Understanding how difficult these temptations are for all believers, the apostle Paul tells us, "Keep a close watch on how you live and on your teaching. Stay true to what is right for the sake of your own salvation and the salvation of those who hear you" (1 Timothy 4:16 NLT).

Staying grounded in God's Word, being prayerful, and having the love, strength, support, and encouragement of fellow believers is extremely important in combatting the temptations that surround us every day. "See to it, brothers and sisters, that none of you has a sinful, unbelieving heart that turns away from the living God," writes the author of Hebrews. "But encourage one another daily, as long as it is called 'Today,' [while there is still time] so that none of you may be hardened by sin's deceitfulness" (Hebrews 3:12-13, emphasis mine).

Despite our best efforts, sin can and does still manage to work its way into the lives of even the most steadfast believers. Regrettably, we have all seen how Satan has successfully taken down even some of our most highly regarded pastors and Bible teachers. Pride, greed, sex, and money have caused many otherwise faithful Christians to fall. As such, we must always be on our guard and lovingly watch out for one another.

If one of our fellow believers does fall into sin or strays from God's truth, we must do everything we can to help restore them to a right relationship with Him. That means being honest and forthright about their sin; yet, loving, compassionate, and respectful when confronting them. If we should find ourselves in this situation, the apostle Paul offers us both wise instruction and words of caution: "Dear brothers and sisters, if another believer is overcome by some sin, you who are godly should gently and humbly help that person back onto the right path. And be careful not to fall into the same temptation yourself" (Galatians 6:1 NLT, emphasis mine).

Paul's admonition to be careful not to fall into temptation ourselves is a critical one. Even if we are not tempted to commit the same sin as a fellow believer, it is quite easy for us to find ourselves falling into other sins. We may feel smug, self-righteous, prideful, or arrogant because we believe we could never fall prey to the same sin to which our brother or sister has fallen. We might find ourselves being so judgmental, demeaning, harshly critical, or condemning that we cause real hurt or harm to the person we are supposed to be restoring. And, sadly, we may become blatantly unloving, unkind, or unforgiving. All these actions lead *us* directly into sin.

Our desired outcome in addressing the sin of a fellow believer must always be to restore them to a loving, faithful, and obedient relationship with their Savior – not to devastate, demoralize, or destroy them for their failure. Therefore, whenever a fellow believer is willing to make a sincere effort to change and repents of his or her sin, we must be both loving and forgiving rather than critical or condemning. The apostle Paul tells us, "Now instead, you ought to forgive and comfort [them], so that [they] will not be overwhelmed by excessive sorrow. I urge you, therefore, to reaffirm your love for [them]" (2 Corinthians 2:7-8, emphasis mine).

Helping fellow believers turn away from sin and back to a faithful and obedient relationship with God is not only an act of love, but it is also vital for their salvation. James, the brother of our Lord Jesus, clarifies this, stating, "My brothers and sisters, if one of you should wander from the truth and someone should bring that person back, remember this: Whoever turns a sinner from the error of their way *will save them from death* and cover over a multitude of sins" (James 5:19-20, emphasis mine).

BE CAREFUL TO LIVE PROPERLY AMONG YOUR UNBELIEVING NEIGHBORS. THEN EVEN IF THEY ACCUSE YOU OF DOING WRONG, THEY WILL SEE YOUR HONORABLE BEHAVIOR, AND THEY WILL GIVE HONOR TO GOD WHEN HE JUDGES THE WORLD (1 PETER 2:12 NLT, emphasis mine).

Turning any person away from sin and pointing them toward a right relationship with Christ Jesus is quite literally a matter of life or death. Consequently, as crucial as it is for us to reflect our Savior's love to our fellow believers, it is equally, or perhaps even more important, for us to model His love to those who do not know who God is or have yet to accept Jesus as their personal Savior. The apostle Paul observes, "For we [Christians] are to God the fragrance of Christ among those who are being saved [believers] and among those who are perishing [unbelievers]" (2 Corinthians 2:15 NKJV, emphasis mine).

In the Garden of Gethsemane on the night our Lord Jesus was taken captive, He fervently prayed that unbelievers would come to know and believe in Him through believers who would share His love and the gospel message with them. "My prayer is not for them [believers] alone," implores our Savior. "I pray also for those who will believe in me through their message, that all of them may be one, Father, just as you are in me and I am in you. May they also be in us so that the world may believe that you have sent me" (John 17:20-21, emphasis mine).

For each one of us, as believers, to be *in* Jesus and our heavenly Father means that we must be living faithful and obedient lives and modeling loving and Christlike character to others through both our words and our actions. If we are not doing so, it is highly unlikely that anyone would want to hear us share God's Word with them, much less believe anything we have to say about Christ Jesus. For this very reason, the apostle Paul warns, "Be wise in the way you act toward outsiders [unbelievers]; make the most of every opportunity. Let your conversation be always full of grace, seasoned with salt [polite, tasteful, truthful, and inviting], so that you may know how to answer everyone" (Colossians 4:5-6, emphasis mine).

It is truly heartbreaking to me that so many unbelievers reject Jesus out of hand because they have heard or seen self-professing Christians talking and behaving in blatantly unchristlike ways. Whenever we are unloving, unkind, judgmental, unforgiving, harsh, hateful, or engaged in worldly (and therefore hypocritical) behavior, it becomes virtually impossible for us to lead an unsaved person to Christ.

Especially in our world today where, tragically, so many self-professed Christians and Christian leaders are linked to physical and sexual abuse, criminal conduct, violence, bigotry, false teachings, and blatantly unchristlike behavior, the way in which we present ourselves as faithful followers of Christ Jesus could not be more important. In an open letter to all Christians, the renowned author and scholar, Os Guinness, wrote: "In a day when religion is tied to hatred and violence – we must show love. In a day of mediocrity and corruption – we must be a people of integrity and excellence".

A well-lived life that continually demonstrates genuine Christlike love and character is essential if we are to have a compelling and believable Christian witness. Having said this, however, we must remember that no matter how loving and faithful our witness for Jesus may be, there will always be people who will reject us as followers of Christ and refuse to hear what we have to say. When we experience this, we must follow the example Jesus set for us when He encountered the same kind of rejection Himself.

The apostle Mark tells us about one such experience our Lord had with a wealthy young man who asked Jesus what he needed to do to inherit eternal life. The young man and Jesus had a brief discussion about obeying the commandments, and the young man told Jesus that he had kept all the commandments since he was a boy. Mark then recalls, "Looking at the man, Jesus felt genuine love for him. 'There is still one thing you haven't done,' [Jesus] told him. 'Go and sell all your possessions and give the money to the poor, and you will have treasure in heaven. Then come, follow me.' At this the man's face fell, and he went away sad, for he had many possessions" (Mark 10:21-22 NLT, emphasis mine).

Even though Jesus dearly loved this young man, wanted him to become one of His followers, and inherit the eternal life he desired Jesus didn't run after him or try to change his mind when the young man rejected Him. Jesus didn't try to reason with him, cajole or coerce him, or attempt to scare him into following Him by threatening him with the dire consequences of the fatal choice he had just made. Jesus respectfully let him go – and kept on loving him.

Throughout His life on earth, our Savior continually presented Himself to people to believe in Him; yet, He never forced Himself on anyone. He knew when to walk away from those who could not, or would not, accept Him. In the same way, when someone rejects us as Christians or refuses to hear or accept the gospel message, we must follow the example Jesus set for us and *lovingly* let them go.

Lovingly letting someone go doesn't mean we stop caring or give up on them. It means we continue to love them, demonstrate Christlike conduct and character toward them, and pray for their hearts to be open to the Holy Spirit's leading. Over time, they may come to see something in us that compels them to want what we have through our relationship with Christ Jesus. A word of caution: we are never likely to win someone to Christ by overtly, or even subtly, trying to impose our beliefs on them, belittling them, behaving in an unkind or superior manner, or ostracizing them. Alternatively, we should radiate our Lord's love, joy, peace, and gracious goodwill so vibrantly and consistently that others will see how wonderful it is and desire what we have for themselves.

KEEP YOUR TONGUE FROM EVIL AND YOUR LIPS FROM SPEAKING LIES (1 PETER 3:10)

Our words are enormously powerful. They can do great good or cause irreparable harm. James, our Lord's brother, uses the following illustrations to help us better understand just how significant the impact of our words can be, and how they can affect our lives and the lives of others for good or evil.

"We can make a large horse go wherever we want by means of a small bit in its mouth. And a small rudder makes a huge ship turn wherever the pilot chooses to go, even though the winds are strong. In the same way, the tongue is a small thing that makes grand speeches. But a tiny spark can set a great forest on fire. And the tongue is a flame of fire. It is a whole world of wickedness, corrupting your entire body. It can set your whole life on fire, for it is set on fire by hell itself. People can tame all kinds of animals, birds, reptiles, and fish, but no one can tame the tongue. It is restless and evil, full of deadly poison. Sometimes it praises our Lord and Father, and sometimes it curses those who have been made in the image of God. And so blessing and cursing come pouring out of the same mouth. Surely, my brothers and sisters, this is not right!" (James 3:3-10 NLT)

I can't imagine what James would think if he walked into a school, shopping mall, or restaurant today and listened to the children, teenagers, and adults carelessly cursing and swearing as they engage in casual conversation. Turning on a television program or watching a movie would surely have shocked and incensed our Lord's brother beyond what he could bear. I know it does me! Sadly, profanity, hate speech, lying, gossiping, speaking falsely, disparaging and damaging people's reputations has become appallingly commonplace.

However, as we learned in the previous chapter, Jesus views the words we speak as an unmistakable indication of our real character; a mirror, so to speak, that reflects our fundamental nature. He declares, "The mouth speaks what the heart is full of. The good man brings good things out of the good stored up in him, and an evil man brings evil things out of the evil stored up in him" (Matthew 12:34-35). Our Lord then goes on to warn us that we will be held accountable for everything we say: "I tell you that everyone will have to give account on the day of judgment for every empty word they have spoken. For by your words you will be acquitted, and by your words you will be condemned" (Matthew 12:36-37). What we say matters profoundly!

When I was a little girl my mother used to say, "If you can't say something nice, don't say anything at all." They were wise words then, and they are wise words now, especially for the followers of Christ Jesus. We would all be wise to pray, as King David did, "May these words of my mouth and this meditation of my heart be pleasing in your sight, Lord, my Rock and my Redeemer" (Psalm 19:14).

IF IT IS POSSIBLE, AS FAR AS IT DEPENDS ON YOU, LIVE AT PEACE WITH EVERYONE (ROMANS 12:18)

In 2008 I attended the Peace Through Understanding conference in Cairo, Egypt. During a panel discussion, one of the participants stated he did not foresee that peace would be possible in the Middle East "until the pain of war is greater than the pain of peace." His view was that the compromises and concessions necessary to achieve peace would have to be less costly, or less painful, than the devastation and lives lost fighting a war. It is difficult for me to comprehend that anyone would find peace more painful than war, yet, as we know, many people feel this way.

As the followers of Christ Jesus, however, our lives must be devoted to seeking peace because, as the apostle Paul reminds us, "God has called us to live in peace" (1 Corinthians 7:15). We learned in Chapter Four that we are given the peace of our Lord and Savior through the Holy Spirit. We must make every effort to live in that peace, not only with fellow believers but with all people. "Make every effort to live in peace with everyone and to be holy," encourages the author of Hebrews (Hebrews 12:14).

When we face conflicts, differences, or even direct attacks, we must do our best to promote peaceful outcomes whenever it is within our power to do so. "Search for peace, and work to maintain it" directs the apostle Peter (1 Peter 3:11, NLT).

Maintaining peaceful relationships with fellow believers is especially important because if we are not living in peace with one another, we will have a tough time promoting peace among others. "Let us therefore make every effort to do what leads to peace and to mutual edification," writes the apostle Paul. "Let the peace of Christ rule in your hearts, since as members of one body you were called to peace" (Romans 14:19; Colossians 3:15). Bearing with one another in love always goes a long way toward achieving peace.

Although we understand that there cannot be true peace on earth until our Lord Jesus returns, we must continue to use all possible means, as outlined in Scripture, to achieve peace whenever it is within our ability to do so. However, if someone is unwilling to make peace, it is best to withdraw from the situation and pray instead for their change of heart. We cannot force peace upon others against their will. Nevertheless, as Jesus' brother, James, tells us, "Peacemakers who sow in peace reap a harvest of righteousness" (James 3:18).

DO NOT BE PROUD, BUT WILLING TO ASSOCIATE WITH PEOPLE OF LOW POSITION (ROMANS 12:16)

"My dear brothers and sisters, how can you claim to have faith in our glorious Lord Jesus Christ if you favor some people over others?" asks our Lord's brother James. "For example, suppose someone comes into your meeting dressed in fancy clothes and expensive jewelry, and another comes in who is poor and dressed in dirty clothes. If you give special attention and a good seat to the rich person, but you say to the poor one, 'You can stand over there, or else sit on the floor' – well, doesn't this discrimination show that your judgments are guided by evil motives?" (James 2:1-4 NLT)

The evil motives that foster discrimination include pride, jealousy, superiority, arrogance, hatefulness, and a lack of love. As such, James goes on to tell us very forthrightly, "If you favor some people over others, you are committing a sin. You are guilty of breaking the law" (James 2:9 NLT). You may be wondering what law is broken when we discriminate. The answer is the law, or commandment, that clearly states we are to love others as ourselves and as Jesus loved us, without regard to race, religion, physical or mental capacity, social class, poverty, wealth, or gender.

The apostle Paul further reminds us that, as our Lord's followers, "In Christ Jesus you are all children of God through faith, for all of you who were baptized into Christ have clothed yourselves with Christ. There is neither Jew nor Gentile, neither slave nor free, nor is there male and female, for you are all one in Christ Jesus" (Galatians 3:26-28).

Love is the great equalizer; it values the life of each person without bias, prejudice, or preference. It sees the good in all people and focuses on their potential as God's creation. As King Solomon so wisely states, "The Lord is the maker of [us] all" (Proverbs 22:2 NKJV, emphasis mine).

DO NOT REPAY ANYONE EVIL FOR EVIL (ROMANS 12:17)

King Solomon warns us against attempting to pay others back

for wrongs that may have been committed against us: "Do not say, 'I'll do to them as they have done to me; I'll pay them back for what they did'" (Proverbs 24:29). Instead, the apostle Peter instructs us to take another path altogether: "Do not repay evil with evil or insult with insult. On the contrary, repay evil with blessing, because to this you were called so that you may inherit a blessing" (1 Peter 3:9).

It can be especially challenging to follow these directives when we or someone we care for has been insulted, humiliated, or suffered a damaging personal affront. It is even more difficult when we or someone we care for are the victims of a truly evil act. Evil takes many forms in this broken world, and those such as torture, rape, and murder, along with physical and psychological abuse are among the most devastating. Many people, understandably, want the perpetrator to be paid back in kind, to suffer, or feel the same kind of pain they feel.

Nevertheless, retaliation, or payback, is never an acceptable answer. It doesn't bring about justice, and it leads to sin – *our* sin. Instead, the apostle Peter reminds us that we must "turn away from evil and do good" (1 Peter 3:11). As difficult as it may be, we must leave room for God's justice to prevail. We must also bear in mind that mercy and forgiveness are mandates of love, and even in the most horrific circumstances, it is possible to show love to others and bless them through the power of the Holy Spirit working within us.

Helping one another remember that we are called to live in love, even with our enemies, is crucial for us, as Christians. As such, the apostle Paul tells us, "Make sure that nobody pays back wrong for wrong, but always strive to do what is good for each other [fellow believers] and for everyone else [unbelievers]" (1 Thessalonians 5:15, emphasis mine).

DO NOT TAKE REVENGE (ROMANS 12:19)

When the desire to repay evil for evil, or even insult for insult, goes unchecked the craving for revenge is usually not far behind. Revenge seeks vengeance at its heart and looks for ways to inflict pain, cause suffering, and do harm – all of which lead us directly into sin. Instead, the apostle Paul tells us to "leave room for God's wrath, for it is written: 'It is mine to avenge; I will repay,' says the Lord. On the contrary: 'If your enemy is hungry, feed him; if he is thirsty, give him something to drink. In doing this, you will heap burning coals on his head'" (Romans 12:19-20).

Paul reminds us that God will not fail to both judge and avenge every wrong; and that this is His role, not ours. Instead, we are to be exceptionally kind to our enemies. Paul's expression, "heap burning coals on his head," is similar to our modern phrase "kill them with kindness." Both have the same goal in mind: that demonstrating exceptional lovingkindness to someone who has done something against us will prick their conscience, convict their spirit, cause them to repent, and perhaps, instill within them the desire to make amends.

However, even if our enemies refuse to repent, we must always leave it up to God to deal with them. King David advises, "Be still before the Lord and wait patiently for him; do not fret when people succeed in their ways, when they carry out their wicked schemes. Refrain from anger and turn from wrath; do not fret – it leads only to evil. For those who are evil will be destroyed, but those who hope in the Lord will inherit the land" (Psalm 37:7-9).

DO NOT JUDGE OTHERS AND YOU WILL NOT BE JUDGED (MATTHEW 7:1)

Jesus tells us forthrightly, "You will be treated as you treat others. The standard you use in judging is the standard by which you will be judged" (Matthew 7:2 NLT). We all tend to look at others and see their flaws and failures without first looking at our own behavior. The apostle Paul, understanding this tendency, writes: "You, therefore, have no excuse, you who pass judgment on someone else, for at whatever point you judge another, you are condemning yourself, because you who pass judgment do the same things. Now we know that God's judgment against those who do such things is based on truth. So when you, a mere human being, pass judgment on them and yet do the same things, do you think you will escape God's judgment?" (Romans 2:1-3). Before we attempt to judge anyone else's behavior, it is always wise to first make an honest assessment of our own.

We must also be careful when judging other's behavior, even that of fellow believers, because while we can see someone's outward conduct, we often don't know what's going on in their hearts, minds, or lives. Gordon-Conwell Theological Seminary professor, Dr. Richard Lovelace once said, "It is very difficult to tell the difference between wolves in sheep's clothing and very confused, very broken, very angry sheep."

Our Lord Jesus declares, "Stop judging by mere appearances, but instead judge correctly" (John 7:24). Correctly judging means taking the time to consider the situation and person carefully, wisely, and lovingly. And while we have a responsibility to be discerning and to determine, or judge, whether an *act or action* is inappropriate or sinful; we may never judge *the person*: their heart, mind, motives, or state of sinfulness – things only God can know and, therefore, judge rightly.

MARRIAGE SHOULD BE HONORED BY ALL (HEBREWS 13:4)

I have often heard people pick and choose specific verses, or even partial verses, of Scripture regarding marital relationships to suit their own ends. For centuries there have been concerns over dominance and submission, husbands ruling over their wives and wives forced into subservient roles. However, in these ongoing debates and discussions, there is one essential truth that seems to keep getting lost or being left out. It is the fact that our Lord Jesus' commandment to love one another as He loves us leaves *no one* out – not husbands or wives.

Bearing this in mind, let's look at a few of the most well-known Scripture verses that speak to husbands and wives. "Wives, submit to your own husbands as you do to the Lord," writes the apostle Paul. "For the husband is the head of the wife as Christ is the head of the church, his body, of which he is the Savior. Now as the church submits to Christ, so also wives should submit to their husbands in everything. Husbands, love your wives, just as Christ loved the church and gave himself up for her ... In this same way, husbands ought to love their wives as their own bodies. He who loves his wife loves himself. After all, no one ever hated his own body, but they feed and care for their body, just as Christ does the church ... Each one of you also must love his wife as he loves himself, and the wife must respect her husband" (Ephesians 5:22-25, 28-29, 33).

While Paul is doing his best to offer good counsel to both husbands and wives, addressing love and respect as well as, establishing headship, the bottom line is still this: In Christ Jesus, we are all equal. He loves us all the same. He wants us to love each other as He loved us: sacrificially, patiently, compassionately, gently, graciously, peaceably, with loving-kindness, and forgiveness. Although Paul did not explicitly tell wives to love their husbands in his directives, our Lord Jesus effectively did so when He issued the command to love one another as He loved us. It is clear that both husbands and wives are to love each other sacrificially, just as Christ Jesus loves His church.

Considering our Lord's commandment to love one another as He loved us, it is imperative that we use care when interpreting the apostle Paul's directive for wives to *submit to*, (or in some translations, obey), *their husbands as they do the Lord because the husband is head of the wife, just as Christ is head of His church*. All too often Paul's qualifier "just as Christ is head of His church" is either dismissed or disregarded. That leads some to wrongly interpret Paul's words to mean that he intends for husbands to rule over their wives with superiority and that the wife is, therefore, subject to her husband's demands. Let's look at a correct interpretation that considers Paul's qualifier.

As we determined above, (and throughout this book), as head of His church, our Lord and Savior's leadership role has always been one of supreme love, righteousness, and self-sacrifice. He wants nothing but the absolute best for us, even to the point of laying down His life to save us. When a husband loves his wife with that kind of love and is a faithful follower of Christ Jesus, he will love his wife selflessly, putting her needs ahead of his own, and want what is best for her. A wife, who is so loved and cherished, (and loves her husband with the same kind of sacrificial love), would not need to submit to her husband out of mandated subservience. Instead, she would willingly be his partner, (as God intended when He created Eve for Adam), holding him in the highest regard, and loving him as selflessly as he loves her.

CHILDREN ARE A HERITAGE FROM THE LORD (PSALM 127:3)

My husband and I have a blended family. I had three sons, and my husband had three sons and a daughter. We have each lost a son. My firstborn son, Wesley, died of a congenital heart defect when he was less than one week old. My stepson, Christopher, tragically died a few years ago at the age of twenty-two. I don't know of pain more excruciating than that of losing a child. Children are a priceless and precious gift from God and should be loved and cherished every day we are blessed to have them in our lives.

As followers of Christ Jesus, our children also fall under the mandate to love one another as Jesus loved us, but with some additional provisions. While we must demonstrate selflessness, loving-kindness, gentleness, compassion, patience, and forgiveness toward our children, they also need nurturing, instruction, protection, and discipline.

Our heavenly Fathers tells us, "These commandments that I give you are to be on your hearts. Impress them on your children" (Deuteronomy 6:6-7). "Discipline your children," writes an author of Proverbs, "and they will give you peace; they will bring you the delights you desire" (Proverbs 29:17). The apostle Paul counsels, "[Parents] do not exasperate your children; instead, bring them up in the training and instruction of the Lord

... Encouraging, comforting, and [urging them] to live lives worthy of God ... Do not embitter your children, or they will become discouraged" (Ephesians 6:4; 1 Thessalonians 2:11-12, Colossians 3:21, emphasis mine).

The apostle Paul also offers these words of instruction to children, stating, "Children, obey your parents in the Lord, for this is right. 'Honor your father and mother' – which is the first commandment with a promise – 'so that it may go well with you and that you may enjoy long life on the earth'" (Ephesians 6:1-3). King Solomon wisely counsels, "My child, listen when your father corrects you. Don't neglect your mother's instruction. What you learn from them will crown you with grace and be a chain of honor around your neck" (Proverbs 1:8-9).

Our children not only learn what we teach them, they learn by the example we set for them. When my sons were small, I had a plaque that said, "Children learn best what they live." Our children observe us constantly – even when we don't think they notice, or listen, they do; and what they see and hear helps shape who they become. They notice when we are consistent, and they notice when we are hypocritical. They notice when we don't "practice what we preach" and they notice if there is sin or wrongdoing in our lives.

Jesus has a dire warning for anyone who leads a child away from Him and into sin. He declares, "If anyone causes one of these little ones – those who believe in me – to stumble, it would be better for them if a large millstone were hung around their neck and they were thrown into the sea" (Mark 9:42). So precious are children to Him, that our Lord sees death as just punishment for leading even one of them away from Him or causing them to sin.

Teaching our children to know and love the Lord, to respect and honor us as their parents, and to love others as Jesus loves them will surely bring both joy and blessing to our children and to us.

DO TO OTHERS AS YOU WOULD HAVE THEM DO TO YOU (LUKE 6:31)

Although many additional Scripture verses teach us how to put true (agape) love into action, Jesus graciously gives us one that covers virtually all of them. He states plainly, "So in everything, do to others what you would have them do to you" (Matthew 7:12). In this verse, commonly known as the Golden Rule, our Lord is telling us once again, in a very straightforward way, that in everything we do and say, we must love our neighbors both as we love ourselves and as He loves us. This means we never treat anyone in a way we don't want someone to treat us or talk to others in a way we wouldn't want someone to speak to us. More importantly, it means never talking to others or treating them any differently than we would Jesus Himself.

Jesus, using the following analogy, explains it like this: "When the Son of Man comes in his glory, and all the angels with him, then he will sit upon his glorious throne. All the nations will be gathered in his presence, and he will separate the people as a shepherd separates the sheep from the goats. He will place the sheep at his right hand and the goats at his left. Then the King will say to those on the right, 'Come, you who are blessed by my Father, inherit the Kingdom prepared for you from the creation of the world. For I was hungry, and you fed me. I was thirsty, and you gave me a drink. I was a stranger, and you invited me into your home. I was naked, and you gave me clothing. I was sick, and you cared for me. I was in prison, and you visited me.'

"Then these righteous ones will reply, 'Lord, when did we ever see you hungry and feed you? Or thirsty and give you something to drink? Or a stranger and show you hospitality? Or naked and give you clothing? When did we ever see you sick or in prison, and visit you?' And the King will say, 'I tell you the truth, when you did it to one of the least of these my brothers and sisters, you were doing it to me!'

"Then the King will turn to those on the left and say, 'Away with you,

you cursed ones, into the eternal fire prepared for the devil and his demons! For I was hungry, and you didn't feed me. I was thirsty, and you didn't give me a drink. I was a stranger, and you didn't invite me into your home. I was naked, and you didn't give me clothing. I was sick and in prison, and you didn't visit me.'

"Then they will reply, 'Lord, when did we ever see you hungry or thirsty or a stranger or naked or sick or in prison, and not help you?' And he will answer, 'I tell you the truth, when you refused to help the least of these my brothers and sisters, you were refusing to help me.' And they will go away into eternal punishment, but the righteous will go into eternal life" (Matthew 25:31-46 NLT).

The hope we all look forward to is eternal life in the presence of our loving Lord and Savior, and the day He says to us, "Well done, good and faithful servant!" (Matthew 25:21). However, until that day, and for as long as we remain on this earth, we, and every other person we meet, still want to experience true (agape) love in our lives. Every one of us wants to be loved selflessly, with kindness, gentleness, patience, compassion, humility, and forgiveness. Each of us wants others to bear with our shortcomings, be respectful and honorable toward us, do right by us, speak kindly and truthfully to us, live peaceably with us, and genuinely care about us. We all need and want this kind of love in our lives – and, ultimately, so does every other person in this broken, sin-filled world.

A Word

"This is the message that you heard from the beginning, that we should love one another" (1 John 3:11 NKJV).

And A Prayer

"May our Lord Jesus Christ himself and God our Father, who loved us and by his grace gave us eternal encouragement and good hope, encourage your hearts and strengthen you in every good deed and word" (2 Thessalonians 2:16-17).

CHAPTER SEVEN
LOVE: A COMMAND AND A COMMISSION

THERE IS ONE MORE ACT OF LOVE, perhaps the most imperative act of love, that Jesus requires of His faithful followers. This vital, life-changing act of love is sometimes known as our "Great Commission." This commission, or command, was first issued by our Lord and Savior to His closest disciples and then, through Scripture, to all the rest of us. "[Jesus] said to them, 'Go into all the world and preach the gospel to all creation. Whoever believes and is baptized will be saved, but whoever does not believe will be condemned'" (Mark 16:15-16, emphasis mine).

The apostle Peter, one of the first recipients of our Lord's commission, explains, "We apostles are witnesses of all [Jesus] did throughout Judea and in Jerusalem. They put him to death by hanging him on a cross, but God raised him to life on the third day. Then God allowed him to appear, not to the general public, but to us whom God had chosen in advance to be his witnesses. We were those who ate and drank with him after he rose from the dead. And he ordered us to preach everywhere and to testify that

Jesus is the one appointed by God to be the judge of all—the living and the dead. He is the one all the prophets testified about, saying that everyone who believes in him will have their sins forgiven through his name" (Acts 10:39-43 NLT, emphasis mine).

These words of Scripture make it clear that Christ Jesus is the only way for any person to receive forgiveness of their sins and eternal life. While this may not be the politically correct message people want to hear today, it is, nonetheless, still true. "Salvation is found in no one else," the apostle Peter assures us, "for there is no other name under heaven given to mankind by which we must be saved" (Acts 4:12). Our Lord and Savior, while praying to His heavenly Father, states explicitly, "Now this is eternal life: that they know you, the only true God, and Jesus Christ, whom you have sent" (John 17:3).

Fulfilling his own commission for others to know Jesus, the apostle Paul writes, "I passed on to you what was most important and what had also been passed on to me. Christ died for our sins, just as the Scriptures said. He was buried, and he was raised from the dead on the third day, just as the Scriptures said. He was seen by Peter and then by the Twelve. After that, he was seen by more than 500 of his followers at one time, most of whom are still alive, though some have died. Then he was seen by James and later by all the apostles. Last of all, as though I had been born at the wrong time, I also saw him" (1 Corinthians 15:3-8 NLT).

This gospel message or "good news," of our Lord and Savior's sacrifice and resurrection for the forgiveness of our sins and the promise of everlasting life is what Jesus commissioned His disciples to share with the whole world. As His disciples did so, they, in turn, passed our Lord's commission on to the next generation of His true followers. The apostle Paul, when passing on the Great Commission to his young protégé Timothy, instructs, "You have heard me teach things that have been confirmed by many reliable witnesses. Now teach these truths to other trustworthy people who will be able to pass them on to others" (2

Timothy 2:2 NLT). These "others" include all the faithful followers of Christ Jesus from Paul's time to the end of time so that every generation will have an opportunity to know Jesus as their Lord and Savior. Having said this, I am aware that there is a prevailing school of thought among many believers that sharing the gospel message and leading others to know Jesus as their Lord and Savior should exclusively be the work of pastors, Bible teachers, church leaders, missionaries, etc. This belief, however, is not in line with our Lord Jesus' commands.

SHARING THE GOSPEL OF LOVE

By way of our Lord and Savior's commandment to love others as He loved us, we are all bound to share the same gospel message He shared. What could be more loving and Christlike than sharing with others the message that brings about a personal relationship with our Lord and Savior, the forgiveness of sins, and the only way to eternal life? "This is good," writes the apostle Paul, "and pleases God our Savior, *who wants all people to be saved and to come to a knowledge of the truth*" (1 Timothy 2:3-4, emphasis mine).

Can we be genuinely loving if we are willing to stay silent about our Lord and Savior, knowing that without Him others will perish? Can we rightly call ourselves Jesus' true followers if we don't follow the example He set for us in sharing the gospel message with others? Our Lord's command to put true (agape) love into action not only calls for us to care for the physical and emotional well-being of people we encounter but their spiritual well-being and eternal lives as well.

Today, if we are willing, it is easy to share the love of God and the gospel message with others. We can personally speak with those who are near to us. And now, with the touch of a few buttons, we can communicate electronically with those as far away as the other side of the world. Through personal interaction, modern media, cell phones, and computers we are blessed to have both the means and accessibility to reach people near and far.

Do these wide-ranging capabilities mean we should be walking up to strangers or indiscriminately telling people at the mall or grocery store that Jesus loves them and wants to forgive them? Should we be texting, tweeting, and emailing the gospel message to everyone we can contact? The answer, in most cases, is probably not.

ALLOWING THE HOLY SPIRIT TO GUIDE US

We must always be sensitive to the Holy Spirit's leading when sharing the gospel message with someone. We must be prayerful, asking for God's guidance and direction beforehand. The Lord will open the right doors for us with the right people at the right time. The apostle Paul confirms this when he writes, "Pray for us, too, that God may open a door for our message, so that we may proclaim the mystery of Christ … Pray also for me, that whenever I speak, words may be given me so that I will fearlessly make known the mystery of the gospel … Pray that I may declare it fearlessly, as I should" (Colossians 4:3; Ephesians 6:19-20, emphasis mine).

At times the Lord will direct us to share the gospel or specific Scripture verses with someone. Sometimes He will lead us to pray for someone's heart and mind to become open to receiving Him. And, in some cases, our Lord may direct us to step away from someone altogether. As painful as it can be for us, there are times when God knows that a person isn't ready, or perhaps He knows that their heart is too hard or their mind too closed to hear His Word, believe in Him, or repent and seek salvation. The apostle Paul reminds us, "The god of this age [Satan] has blinded the minds of unbelievers, so that they cannot see the light of the gospel that displays the glory of Christ, who is the image of God" (2 Corinthians 4:4, emphasis mine).

Regardless of which path the Holy Spirit directs us to take, it is always the right thing for us to continue to pray for the salvation of every unsaved person, both those close to us and those throughout the world.

Having said this, some of us may have been praying for someone for a long time or felt called to witness to someone specifically, yet that person has not accepted Jesus as their Savior. This can be disheartening and frustrating, especially if that person is a beloved family member or a close friend. However, we must remember that even though we have been commissioned to share the gospel with others, it is not up to us to "save" anyone. Only God can do that through the working of the Holy Spirit in a person's heart. Jesus tells us, "No one can come to me unless the Father who sent me draws them to me" (John 6:44 NLT). We can, and should, continue to pray for and share the gospel with people as the Holy Spirit leads us; but with the understanding that it is ultimately up to Him to convict the person's heart and up to the person to invite Jesus into their life.

ALWAYS MODELING THE WAY TO CHRIST

Whether we are called to witness to someone or to wait and pray for them, we must continue to demonstrate Christlike conduct and character in every circumstance. As we have already come to understand, if we are not communicating God's love and conveying Christlike character, it will be very difficult, if not impossible, for us to interest anyone in what we have to say about our Lord and Savior.

America's beloved pastor, Dr. Charles Stanley, often reminds his listeners to look their best, do their best, and be their best. He knows that our Christian witness is seen in all that we are as well as, in everything we do and say. It is evident in our facial expressions, body language, temperament, the way we dress, how we act, and how we communicate – especially during challenging or stressful situations. As we have already come to understand, everything we present to the world around us as the followers of Christ Jesus, be it favorable or unfavorable, becomes a reflection of our Lord and Savior to those around us.

Saying this reminds me of a catchphrase commonly used today that declares, "preach the gospel and if necessary, use words." This expression conveys the idea that if we live good lives and display Christlike conduct and character our example should be enough for others to know Jesus without our having to tell them about Him. As appealing as it sounds, however, this concept is wholly inaccurate and counter to the teachings of Scripture.

THE ONLY WAY TO KNOW JESUS

The apostle Paul explains, "If you declare with your mouth, 'Jesus is Lord,' and believe in your heart that God raised him from the dead, you will be saved. For it is with your heart that you believe and are justified, and it is with your mouth that you profess your faith and are saved … Everyone who calls on the name of the Lord will be saved … How, then, can [unbelievers] call on the one they have not believed in? And how can they believe in the one of whom they have not heard? And how can they hear without someone preaching to them … Consequently, faith comes from hearing the message, and the message is heard through the word about Christ" (Romans 10:9-10, 13-14, 17, emphasis mine).

The only way people are going to know who God is, who their Lord and Savior is, and how they can be saved is when someone loves and cares enough about them and their eternal destiny to tell them. King David clearly understood the importance of telling others about the love of God as he confesses: "I have told all your people about your justice. I have not been afraid to speak out, as you, O Lord, well know. I have not kept the good news of your justice hidden in my heart; I have talked about your faithfulness and saving power. I have told everyone in the great assembly of your unfailing love and faithfulness" (Psalm 40:9-10 NLT).

God places many people in our paths as we go through life, providing us with innumerable opportunities to make a difference in their lives. Our willingness to be obedient to His commands and to reach out to others with His love may mean the difference between someone dying in their sins or finding forgiveness, salvation, and eternal life. As such, sharing the gospel message, demonstrating the love of Christ, and lifting others up in prayer are essential and priceless acts of love.

FACING PERSECUTION FOR SHARING GOD'S LOVE

While responding to our Lord's Great Commission and obeying His commandment to live in love can be life-changing and life-saving they can, unfortunately, also be life-threatening. There are hundreds of thousands of Christians around the world being persecuted, imprisoned, tortured, and put to death for faithfully living in God's love, speaking His truth in love, and lovingly sharing the gospel message.

Here in the United States, as well as in many other countries, the persecution of Christians is growing rapidly. I never dreamed I would see such blatant and vicious persecution of Christians in America, witness the removal of the Ten Commandments from public view, see prayer forbidden in public places, or watch as atheists try to have the name of God systematically expunged from United States documents. Great efforts are being made to silence the followers of Christ Jesus, remove our religious freedoms, and rescind our constitutional rights to speak freely and practice our faith. It is heartbreaking, deeply troubling, and, at times, infuriating. However, it is not unexpected.

The apostle Paul reminds us that "In fact, everyone who wants to live a godly life in Christ Jesus will be persecuted … For it has been granted to you on behalf of Christ not only to believe in him, but also to suffer for him" (2 Timothy 3:12; Philippians 1:29). "However, if you suffer as a Christian," writes the apostle Peter, "do not be ashamed, but praise God that you bear that name" (1 Peter 4:16).

Our Lord and Savior was certainly not unaware of the brutal persecution His faithful followers and name bearers would be facing. He acknowledges this when He tells us: "If the world hates you, keep in mind that it hated me first" (John 15:18). Our loving Savior, however, does not leave us to despair over this. Instead, He encourages and reassures us with these words: **"What blessings await you when people hate you and exclude you and mock you and curse you as evil because you follow the Son of Man. When that happens, be happy! Yes, leap for joy! For a great reward awaits you in heaven"** (Luke 6:22-23 NLT). The apostle Peter confirms, "If you are insulted because of the name of Christ, you will be blessed, for the Spirit of glory and of God rests on you" (1 Peter 4:14).

The difficult times we are currently living in only make it that much more crucial for us to persevere in faith, live in God's love, and unashamedly share the gospel message with everyone the Holy Spirit impresses upon our hearts. We must stand firm and proclaim, as the apostle Paul did, "I am not ashamed of the gospel, because it is the power of God that brings salvation to everyone who believes" (Romans 1:16).

Seeking the salvation of the unsaved through the sharing of our love, prayers, and the gospel message is, without question, both an act of loving obedience to our Lord and Savior's commandments and the faithful answering of His call for us to share the gospel message with the world. How wonderful for each of us to be able to say, along with the apostle Paul, "Because we loved you so much, we were delighted to share with you not only the gospel of God but our lives as well" (1 Thessalonians 2:8-9).

FALSE TEACHERS AND FALSE TEACHINGS

I would be remiss if I did not take the time, here, to address those who are perpetuating false gospels and false teachings. Not only are false teachers and misled people leading millions of people away from God, but they are also, sadly, leading many into sinful lifestyles that are completely counter to the Word of God.

The apostle Paul, understanding what was to come, writes, "A time is coming when people will no longer listen to sound and wholesome teaching. They will follow their own desires and will look for teachers who will tell them whatever their itching ears want to hear. They will reject the truth and chase after myths" (2 Timothy 4:3-4 NLT). The apostle's words, spoken centuries ago, certainly couldn't ring any truer than they do today.

Given that people's eternal lives are at stake, we, as the followers of Christ Jesus, cannot afford to allow false teachers and false teachings to go unchecked. "Beware of false prophets who come disguised as harmless sheep but are really vicious wolves," warns Jesus. "You can identify them by their fruit, that is, by the way they act" (Matthew 7:15-16 NLT).

The men and women who misquote, misinterpret, and misapply Scripture and promote false doctrines to suit their own purposes lead countless people away from the Truth and, all too often, into making wrong choices that lead to sinful behaviors. "I urge you, brothers and sisters," counsels the apostle Paul, "to watch out for those who cause divisions and put obstacles in your way that are contrary to the teaching you have learned. Keep away from them. For such people are not serving our Lord Christ, but their own appetites. By smooth talk and flattery they deceive the minds of naïve people" (Romans 16:17-18).

Satan was the proverbial "wolf in sheep's clothing" when he tried to deceive our Lord Jesus and tempt Him into sin in the Judaean desert. Disguising himself as a scholar/theologian, Satan misquoted and misapplied Psalm 91:11 in his failed attempt to lead our Lord into sin. As the great deceiver and father of lies, Satan still uses these same old tactics today, working them out through misdirected human beings, including clergy, biblical scholars, and laypeople.

Our Lord Jesus, of course, knew the actual words of the Scriptures and their true meaning when Satan tried to deceive Him in the desert; and He correctly applied the Word of God to rebuke Satan. Unless we, too, are firmly grounded in the truth of God's Word we may neither recognize nor be able to stand up against false teachers or effectively refute their errors.

The only way for us to know the whole truth of God's Word is to read and study the Holy Scriptures, seek wise counsel from Bible-believing followers of Christ Jesus, and pray continuously for God to give us discernment, guidance, and wisdom. It is also imperative that we test and confirm what is right and true based on God's Word as a whole. Taking a single verse or a few verses of Scripture out of context, or automatically accepting what someone tells us is the correct interpretation or meaning of a Scripture verse or verses, can quickly and easily lead us into error.

Having said this, it is vital for all of us to remember that, as fallible human beings, even the most honorable and well-intentioned Christians can, and sometimes do, make interpretive mistakes. Even Jesus' disciples and the apostle Paul had disputes at times. As such, I strongly encourage you to search the Scriptures, study them carefully, and discuss them with other Bible-believing followers of Christ Jesus. (The same is true for the Scripture verses I have used in the writing of this book.)

As I encourage you to take these steps, I am also acutely aware that with all the resources available today at the touch of a finger, it can be quite challenging to sort through the copious amounts of material and decipher the often-conflicting messages presented to us. We must assess carefully not only what is said, but who is saying it. Along with the many honorable Bible teachers doing their best to help us understand the Scriptures, there are an equal, if not greater, number who are promoting purely worldly views, corrupting the Word of God with errancies and half-truths, and, in some instances, blatantly teaching what is utterly contrary to the Word of God with great conviction.

Bearing this in mind, we must remember that nowhere in Scripture does it ever say, "Feel free to modify the meaning of God's Word to suit your individual agendas, standards, and mindsets" or "Just pick and choose the parts you like and disregard the rest of it." We must never join in with those who participate in these deceptions, perpetuate false teachings, or promote a counterfeit gospel. We must not compromise to please those around us, fit in with the crowd, or be *politically correct*. "On the contrary," writes the apostle Paul, "we [the true followers of Christ

Jesus] speak as those approved by God to be entrusted with the gospel. We are not trying to please people but God, who tests our hearts" (1 Thessalonians 2:4, emphasis mine).

TURNING HEARTS BACK TO GOD

It can be terribly painful to see how far this world has fallen away from God and bought into Satan's destructive lies and deceptions. However, all is not lost. There is still hope! Just as was true of the Israelites when they fell away from God, worshipping their golden idols and rejecting the Lord, it is never too late to repent, turn to God, and receive forgiveness, restoration, and blessing.

The prophet Joel tells us, "That is why the Lord says, 'Turn to me now, while there is time. Give me your hearts. Come with fasting, weeping, and mourning. Don't tear your clothing in your grief, but tear your hearts instead.' Return to the Lord your God, for he is merciful and compassionate, slow to get angry and filled with unfailing love. He is eager to relent and not punish" (Joel 2:12-13 NLT).

The prophet Ezekiel records these powerful words of God: "If wicked people turn away from all their sins and begin to obey my decrees and do what is just and right, they will surely live and not die ... Do you think that I like to see wicked people die? says the Sovereign Lord. No, of course not! I want them to turn from their wicked ways and live ... I take no pleasure in the death of anyone, declares the Sovereign Lord. Repent and live!" (Ezekiel 18:21, 23; 32 NLT).

God longs for every person to believe in Christ Jesus as their Savior, to repent of their sins, be baptized, and receive the gift of eternal life. To that end, God has been and continues to be, extremely patient. As the apostle Peter assures us, "The Lord isn't really being slow about his promise, as some people think. No, he is being patient for your sake. He does not want anyone to be destroyed, but wants everyone to repent" (2 Peter 3:9 NLT).

Of course, our Lord's patience won't last forever, and none of us know when our time on this earth or the world itself will come to an end. Jesus, wanting us to understand this clearly, warns, "About that day or hour no one knows, not even the angels in heaven, nor the Son, but only the Father. Be on guard! Be alert! You do not know when that time will come" (Mark 13:32-33).

LOVE IN THE LAST DAYS

Recognizing that time for all of us is running out, the apostle Peter tells us, "The end of the world is coming soon. Therefore, be earnest and disciplined in your prayers. Most important of all, continue to show deep love for each other, for love covers a multitude of sins. Cheerfully share your home with those who need a meal or a place to stay. God has given each of you a gift from his great variety of spiritual gifts. Use them well to serve one another. Do you have the gift of speaking? Then speak as though God himself were speaking through you. Do you have the gift of helping others? Do it with all the strength and energy that God supplies. Then everything you do will bring glory to God through Jesus Christ" (1 Peter 4:7-11 NLT).

As we take into our hearts the current condition of the world in which we live and the fact that people everywhere are desperately in need of the love, hope, and forgiveness that can only be found through a personal relationship with our heavenly Father and His beloved Son, we must heed the encouraging words of the apostle Paul: "Let us not become weary in doing good, for at the proper time we will reap a harvest if we do not give up" (Galatians 6:9).

BLESSINGS FOR THOSE WHO FOLLOW JESUS

The "harvest" we will reap for loving God and loving others not only includes those who are led to know Jesus as their Savior, but our Lord's promise that "the Son of Man is going to come in his Father's glory with his angels, and then he will reward each person according to what they have done" (Matthew 16:27).

Those of us who love God with all our hearts and do our best to obey His commands and live Christlike lives have received this assurance from our Lord and Savior: "Blessed are all who hear the word of God and put it into practice" (Luke 11:28 NLT). "Blessed are those whose ways are blameless, who walk according to the law of the Lord," writes King David. "Blessed are those who keep his statutes and seek him with all their heart" (Psalm 119:1-2).

In His Sermon on the Mount, Jesus graciously reveals many of these blessings and rewards, stating, "Blessed are the poor in spirit, for theirs is the kingdom of heaven. Blessed are those who mourn, for they will be comforted. Blessed are the meek, for they will inherit the earth. Blessed are those who hunger and thirst for righteousness, for they will be filled. Blessed are the merciful, for they will be shown mercy. Blessed are the pure in heart, for they will see God. Blessed are the peacemakers, for they will be called children of God. Blessed are those who are persecuted because of righteousness, for theirs is the kingdom of heaven" (Matthew 5:3-10). What extraordinary blessings, unsurpassed love, and irrepressible joy belong to the followers of Jesus!

LIVING IN LOVE, CHANGING LIVES

Our gracious, loving God has granted us unwavering, unfailing, unconditional love. He fills our lives with joy, hope, and peace. He guides us, teaches us, and helps us. He meets our needs and blesses us in ways we could never have imagined. He forgives our sins and promises us eternal life through His beloved Son. How can any of us not want to share His extraordinary love and incomparable blessings with the whole world?

Only our Creator and Savior can ultimately change this perilously broken world, and only He can save the lost and sinful people in this world. Knowing the truth of this, and the consequences for all those who remain unredeemed, there has never been a more critical time for us, as the faithful followers of Christ Jesus, to live in God's love, to claim it fully for ourselves, and to share it boldly with others.

Seeking God with all our hearts and doing everything we can to turn the hearts of others to our Lord and Savior is what we, as ambassadors of Christ Jesus and emissaries of almighty God, have been both commanded and commissioned to do. Therefore, as the apostle Paul urgently implores every one of us, "Be on guard. Stand firm in the faith. Be courageous. Be strong. And do everything with love" (1 Corinthians 16:13-14 NLT).

A Word

"Now these three remain: faith, hope and love. But the greatest of these is love" (1 Corinthians 13:13).

And A Prayer

"May the Lord make your love for one another and for all people grow and overflow, just as our love for you overflows. May he, as a result, make your hearts strong, blameless, and holy as you stand before God our Father when our Lord Jesus comes again with all his holy people. Amen" (1 Thessalonians 3:12-13 NLT).

ACKNOWLEDGEMENTS

This book has been a wonderful blessing in my life, as have the many people who helped make it possible. My husband, Jerry, never stopped believing in me or in the Lord's call for me to write this book. Thank you for your steadfast love and support. My son, Bryan Drahota, was my first reader, editor, and an enormous help to me. Thank you for your critiques and encouragement. Without you this book might never have gotten off the ground. My son, Brandon Drahota, through whom I saw first-hand that true love not only endures all things, but also overcomes all things when we trust our Great Healer. My faith and understanding of God's love and grace are stronger because of what we have been through together. My sister, Sherry Rose, whose love, patient support, honest feedback, words of wisdom, and tireless prayers kept me going and gave me strength. Thank you from the bottom of my heart! I am exceedingly grateful to my dear friends Lisa Griffin, Jane Schroeckenstein, and Ron Tortelli for their gracious support, editorial help, and words of encouragement. My thanks also to the many family members, friends, acquaintances, and fellow believers who encouraged, supported, and prayed for me as I sought to fulfill our Lord's call to write this book. I also want to posthumously thank Mary C. Hoff for her great kindness to me when I began writing this book. You are not forgotten.

Above all, my deepest and most heartfelt "thank you" to the God Who is Love. I am truly humbled by, and profoundly grateful for, Your forgiveness, mercy, and grace in placing this call upon my life. There is no greater love than Your love! You are forever my all-in-all.

THANK YOU TO MY READERS

Thank you for taking the time to read this book. It is my sincere hope that it blessed your life and encouraged your heart. You can make an enormous difference in this badly broken world; and our loving and gracious God is ready and waiting to help you make that happen.

I pray that you will grow in the love of Christ Jesus each day, touch the lives of others with His love and yours as you are led by the Holy Spirit, and receive in return our Lord's most abundant blessings all the days of your life.

I welcome your thoughts, ideas, and feedback and look forward to hearing how this book may have impacted your life, your relationship with our Lord and Savior, Jesus Christ, and your relationships with others. Please email your insights and comments to: livinginloveministry@yahoo.com.

Ever grateful God is with us,

Joie Froelich

www.ingramcontent.com/pod-product-compliance
Lightning Source LLC
Chambersburg PA
CBHW052054070526
44584CB00017B/2170